Credit Secret

2 **books on** 1

Credit Secret Theory
Credit Secret Pratical

John Cash - Credit Score Academy

Credit Secret Theory

a complete guide to learning about credit score theory, what it takes to improve it; get your bank loan today.

John Cash - Credit Score Academy

INTRODUCTION 9

WHAT IS THE CREDIT SCORE? 11

WHAT'S GOOD CREDIT SCORE? 15

WHAT'S THE FICO SCORE? 17

WHY IS FICO SCORE IMPORTANT? 20

THE DIFFERENCE BETWEEN FICO AND OTHER CREDIT SCORES 23

HOW IS FICO SCORE CALCULATED? 27

WHY SHOULD I CARE ABOUT HAVING GOOD CREDIT? 32

ACCESS TO BEST CREDIT CARDS 36

EASY ACCESS TO LOAN 39

LOWER INTEREST RATES ON LOANS 41

EASY APPROVAL FOR RENTAL OF HOUSES AND APARTMENT 43

BETTER JOB APPLICATIONS 45

NEGOTIATING POWER 47

WHAT IS IN A CREDIT REPORT? 49

CREDIT REPORTING AGENCIES 57

WHERE DO AGENCIES GET INFORMATION? 62

WHAT'S A GOOD CREDIT SCORE? 67

CONCLUSION 72

Introduction

The reality is that we live in a society that almost demands that we have some form of credit, not to get ahead, but simply to survive. When we are without it, we suffer in more ways than one.

What better reason is there to start mending our financial health than this? Yes, it can be scary, unpredictable, and stressful but by applying the strategies outlined in this book, you can find your way to a successful credit repair without the additional expense of hiring services to do it for you.

There is an excellent benefit to fixing your credit yourself. Not only do you save yourself from an additional expense when you are already financially strapped, but you become an expert and play a major starring role in your own life.

By applying the information in this book, you will have enough resources at your disposal to get your finances back on track. They say that it takes three weeks for you to get into long-lasting habits. When you are able to budget and watch how you spend, you will quickly find yourself developing new habits.

This guidebook will cover all of the tips and tricks that you need to know in order to get to know about credit scores. You can utilize these administrations if you are worried about wholesale fraud, or when you are building your credit profile and you have to screen your advancement. If your requirement for a credit card score is easygoing, you don't have to leave behind month-to-month expenses to pay for an observing help.

What is the credit score?

Credit score is the number derived after analyzing a person's financial records, particularly his credit history, to determine his creditworthiness level. It is a number that represents how well that person handles all the money that he borrows. It is the main determinant used by many lending companies, next to or together with the five C's of credit (character, capacity, capital, collateral, conditions). While the latter determines the creditworthiness of a person, the former objectively interprets it. Most companies use numerous credit assessment measures to assess their potential borrowers' creditworthiness, but the credit score stands to be the most objective of all. Credit scores help many institutions in making financial and corporate decisions. Lending companies such as credit card companies, banks, and other financial institutions use the credit score to determine the possible risks they will face when lending money to a person.

They also use this score to evaluate the possible losses they might experience due to unpaid loans and bad debts. They also use this score to determine who are qualified to be their borrowers, the amount they will lend to them, the different terms and conditions that they may impose for each of them, and the interest rate they can charge to them.

For instance, obtaining credit is a person's option whenever he runs out of cash. He can still buy using a credit card issued by the lending company. However, issuing a credit card takes many steps, one of which is assessing his financial capability. The credit score will help lending companies in determining if he is a creditworthy person.

Creditworthiness is the measure of the possibility that a person will pay his financial obligations. Other countries, however, consider creditworthiness as the measure of the possibility that a person will fail to comply with his monetary obligations.

Creditworthiness is important in financial matters because lending companies also have to generate revenue from lending money. Suppose they do not check the creditworthiness of each of their borrowers. In that case, they may find themselves in bankruptcy either because their borrowers are cashless or because they already have left the country. Creditworthiness serves as a means to protect the interest not only of the lending company, but also of the public.

What's good credit score?

The main document used by lending companies in computing a person's credit score is the credit report. It contains various personal and financial information of the individual such as the place they live, the specific manner through which they pay their bills, their current financial condition (whether they are currently bankrupt or insolvent), and whether they been sued for collection of money due to unpaid loans. Obtaining a credit report is free, so before a person applies for credit, they must get a copy of it. The Fair Credit Reporting Act (FCRA), the law governing the reporting of a person's credit information, requires every credit reporting company or agency to provide a person a free copy of their credit report once every year at their request.

What's the fico score?

You have heard it again and again, your FICO score must be so high to get this type of credit, this kind of interest rate, and this type of privilege. The FICO score is the single most important factor that stands between you and just about anything you want to get. While many people fully understand the impact of the FICO score on their credit, few people, if asked, could actually tell you what it is or how it is determined. Given the weight that this number holds over so many people, it seems amazing that more people don't ask what it is or what they can do about it. They just simply accept the fact that this number has so much power in their lives.

Most people do not realize that the credit bureau that issues your reports does not determine your score, it is done by another company, a third party called the Fair, Isaac Corporation (FICO). They weigh all the different elements of your credit report to determine what number you get. All the data collected by the credit bureaus are factored in to come up with a three-digit number.

Almost every creditor will want to see your FICO score before he decides to give you credit. But knowing what the numbers really mean can make a huge difference in managing and taking back control of your financial future. As you gain more knowledge about how the system works, it can empower you. While other factors will weigh in the decision, anyone whose goal is to improve their creditworthiness needs to start with the FICO score as nearly all credit decisions will be based on it.

One of the first things you should understand is the scoring range so you can see what your number really means.

Why Is Fico Score Important?

This is probably the only grade you should seriously worry about after you get out of school. It is the grade you get for your financial stability. That single three-digit number will tell the world what they should think about you. But it is not a number that reflects only the present it is also a pathway to your future as well. If anything is wrong with your reports, it is your responsibility to get it fixed. This is the primary and most effective way to change it.

For this reason, it is important that you know what's in your report so that you can correct any information that is incorrect or incomplete. This will help to bring your score up higher. Very few people have a perfect score of 950, but you can improve that number if you know what to do.

The Difference Between FICO and Other Credit Scores

The reason for this is that FICO scores will be seen as the standard when it comes to making fair and accurate decisions about an individual's creditworthiness.

Now there are other credit scores out there, and they can be used in some situations. These other scores will calculate the number they give you differently than the FICO score can. So, while it may seem like some of those other scores are similar to what we see with the FICO score, they aren't. Only FICO scores will be used by most of the top lenders you want to borrow from, and while the others can be good for some monitoring of your score, if you would like, the best way to go is with the FICO score.

There are different scores that lenders can get from the different bureaus and the score for one may not mean the same thing as the other. This is important because when you get your credit score, it is imperative that you know exactly what your number means and if you're in hot water or not. There are different credit scoring ranges for different lenders. Here are the most popular ones:

FICO Credit Scoring Range

Extension of Range: 350-850 is the credit score range. The Fair Isaac Corporation's credit score is what many lenders see when they look at your credit report.

This score is one of the most used out there. The FICO score shows how creditworthy you are in the eyes of lenders.

There's not just one type of FICO score as new next generation/NextGen scores have been introduced that go up to 950.

Vantage Score Credit Scoring Range

Extension of Range: 501-990. The Vantage Score credit scoring model is formed by the 3 major credit bureaus, namely TransUnion, Equifax and Experian.

When you receive your credit score from one of these bureaus directly, they will most likely give you this Vantage Score. It is also referred to as the Vantage Score 2.0 model.

Vantage Scores 3.0 Credit Scoring Range

Extension of Range: 300-850. This credit scoring model is largely similar to the previous one (Vantage Score 2.0 Model). The only big difference is that the range is slightly larger for the Vantage Score 3.0 Range, i.e. 300-850.

Trans Risk Credit Scoring Range

Extension of Range: 300-850. This range is used by the credit bureau Trans Union when they are trying to pin your creditworthiness down.

Equifax Credit Scoring Range

Extension of Range: 280-850. This is the scoring range used by the credit bureau Equifax, to show how risky it is to lend to you.

Experian Plus Credit Scoring Range

Extension of Range: 330-830. This one is used by the credit bureau Experian and is how that credit bureau shows how creditworthy you are.

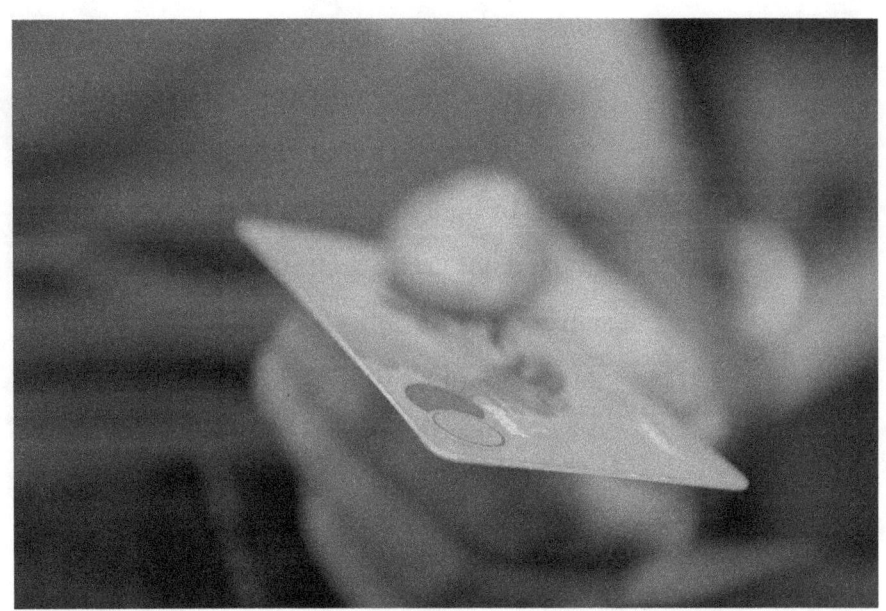

How Is Fico Score Calculated?

When your FICO score is determined, several factors must be taken into consideration. The actual score is calculated based on their order of importance.

35% is based on your payment history. As long as you pay your bills on time, this part of your score will be high.

30% is based on how much money you owe. It is called your credit utilization ratio. While you want to be using your credit, you don't want to be using 100% of it. When you are maxed out credit wise, it can have an impact on how high your score will be. Try to aim to spend no more than 30% of your total credit limit to get an optimal balance.

15% is based on your credit history. The longer you have had credit, the better.

10% is based on the different types of credit you have. A nice combination is always good to see. If you have credit card debt, a mortgage, and installment loans, it shows that you are versatile when it comes to credit and you can handle all sorts of things responsibility.

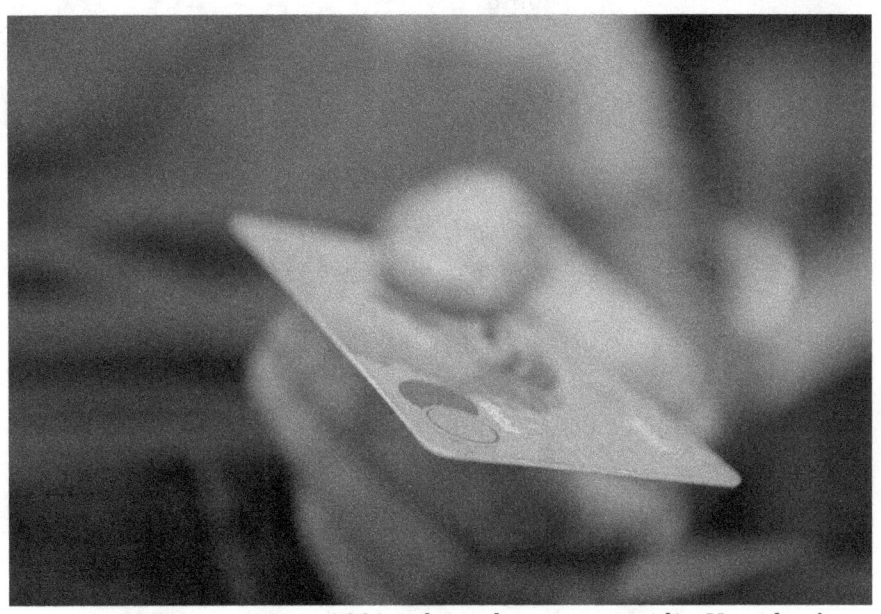

10% is based on new credit. You don't want to go out and apply for a bunch of loans to get new credit, but if you have some new credit, it looks very positive and could have a positive effect on your score.

Having information like this can go a long way in helping you to see what kind of things actually are involved in determining your credit score. As you can see, all of it is important but being able to see exactly where your weak points are can give you a specific target area you can focus on improving.

No one knows the exact formula for calculating a credit score. The Fair Isaacs Corporation is pretty tight-lipped when asked about the specific algorithms they use. However, as you can see from the above, much of the weight is based on your payment history. That's why it is so important that you find a way to pay your bills as soon as they come due. By doing this, you can be sure that you'll have a leg up when it comes to repairing your credit.

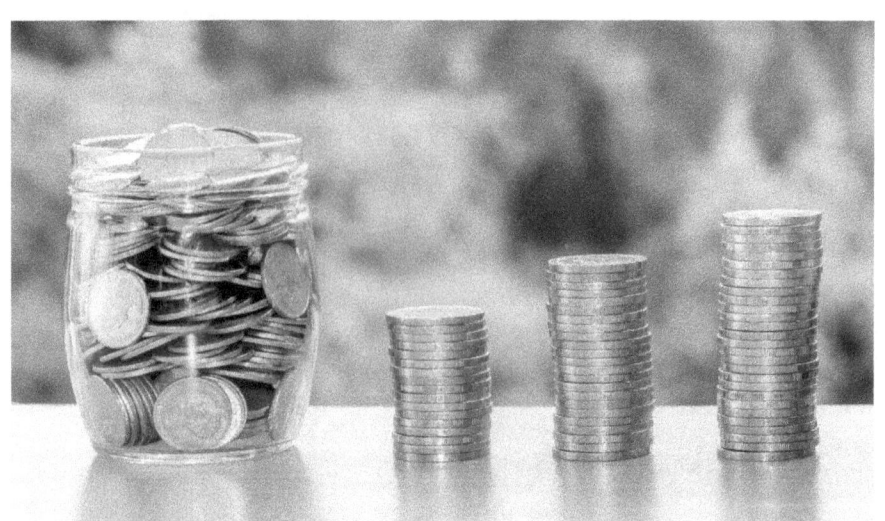

Why should i care about having good credit?

When you apply for credit, insurance, telephone service and even a place to live, providers want to know if you have a good risk level. And to make that decision, they use credit scores.

A credit score is a number. A high score means you have good credit. A low score means you have bad credit.

A higher score means that you represent a lower risk and are more likely to get the product or service - or pay less.

It works as follows: Credit managers extract information from your credit reports, such as your bill payment history, your accounts' age, your unpaid debts and the collection actions initiated against you.

Credit scores can be used in various ways. These are some examples.

- **Insurance companies** use the information in your credit report and combine it with other factors to predict the probability that you present an insurance claim and predict the amount you could claim. They consider this information to decide if they will grant you insurance and how much they will charge you.

- .**Public service companies** use credit scores to decide if they will require a new customer deposit to provide the service. Cell phone providers and homeowners who rent homes also use scores when considering a new client or tenant.

Each type of company has different scoring systems, and credit scoring models can also be based on other information apart from your credit report's data. For example, when you apply for a mortgage loan, the system can consider the amount of the advance, the total amount of your debts and your income.

Access to best credit cards

Having a good credit score is an essential factor to qualify for an opportunity to get a credit card that provides excellent cash-back reward programs, awesome advantages, low rates and so many others. Besides paying lower interest and fees, having access to the best credit card means you can get a larger credit limit. Therefore, you can have freedom and flexibility to make purchases you want without the financial constraint that arises from a small credit limit.

An increase in your credit limit results into an increase in your creditworthiness overtime. This shows banks and other lending institutions that you are mature enough and can handle the responsibility of having access to a large amount of credit.

Having a good credit score can help you discover cards with cash-back rates as high as 5% at different places like restaurants, grocery stores, E-commerce platforms, gas stations and any other time your card is used.

Easy access to loan

Having a bad credit history will make you scared of applying for a new credit card or loan due to the fear of being turned down. Maintaining a good credit score tells a lot about your credit responsibility. When banks and lending institution see your credit score, they can be rest assured that they are not at risk and you are likely to pay back the money you are asking them to loan to you. Though this does not guarantee an outright approval because other factors such as your income, debts, etc. are also considered, it just provides you with a very good chance of getting approval.

Lower interest rates on loans

The interest rate that you get to pay is directly dependent on your credit score. Suppose you have a very good credit score. In that case, you might not need to consider the interest rate when applying for a credit card because you will always qualify for the best interest rates thereby paying very minimal charges on credit card loans. If you always want your interest rate to be low, you need to have a good credit score.

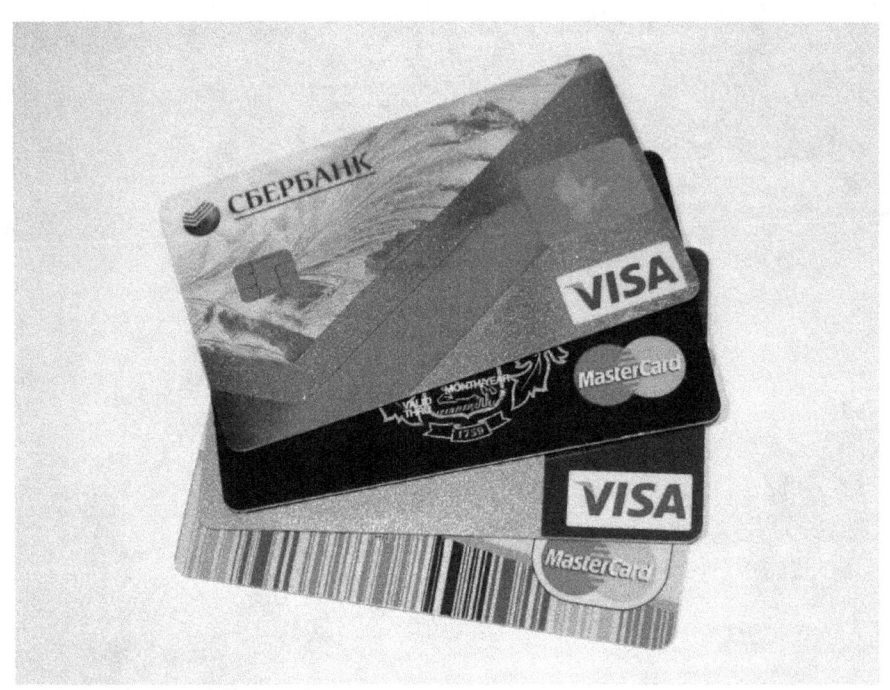

Easy approval for rental of houses and apartment

So many landlords and apartment owners tend to check credit scores for the same reason lenders do routinely. They fear that tenants with bad credit score might be unable to keep up with rent payment and avoid the hassle – they avoid tenants with a high risk. Having previous bad credit scores gives the property owner an unsettled mind that you might not be able to pay back at the stipulated time, a good credit score says otherwise.

Better job applications

This is not the only criteria considered by employers, however, so many employers access the credit history of various job seekers during their application processes especially when the job you're applying for requires handling money or accessing clients' sensitive financial information. Majority of employers believe that your ability to use credit responsibly makes you more likely to be a responsible employee.

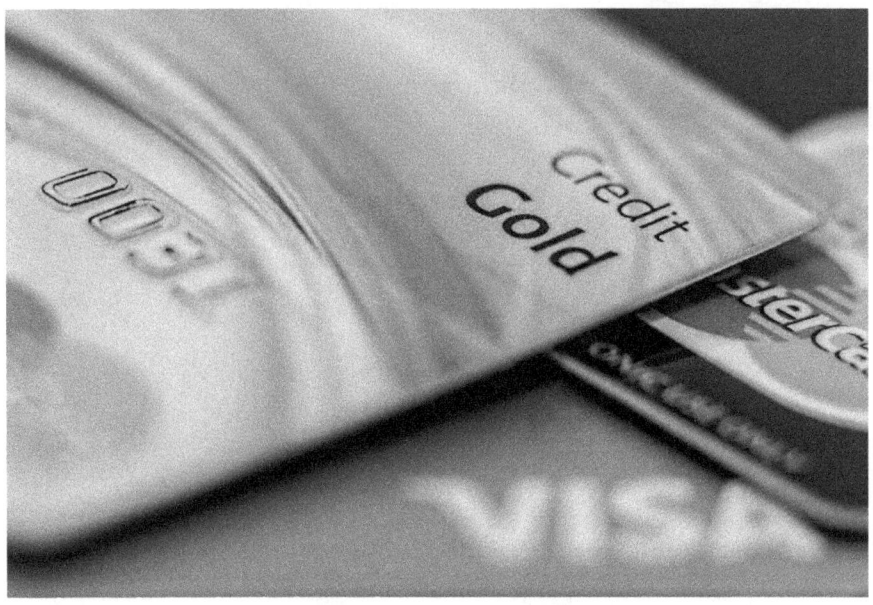

Negotiating Power

You can get leverage to negotiate a lower interest rate on your student loan, new credit card, mortgage and others if you have a good credit score. Having a credit card with a history that doesn't have an iota of problems provides you with more bargaining power, that is needed to secure the favorable terms that you need. You therefore can carefully pick the terms that will be of great advantage to your present financial circumstance.

What is in a credit report?

There are a lot of different categories in the report and that means you need to weigh out different things to make sure that your credit score is high enough for you to get the things you want.

The best scores are those that are over 900 but not many people are able to achieve that. If your score is over a 700 you have good credit and you're pretty much guaranteed any type of credit that you might apply for. But you want to keep in mind that different types of credit card companies or credit

agencies will want a different score.

If your score is in the 600's you have a decent chance of getting credit in most places but not all. This isn't guaranteed, however. There are plenty of agencies that will consider you a little bit of a risk.

Your credit score is an indication of how much of a risk it is to give you credit. When you first start out getting credit you have a low credit score. This tells the person checking your score that there is a high level of risk involved. That's why your score is low. As you get more recorded payments your score will go up because the risk of you not paying for things is getting lower.

Now it's not just late payments or missed payments that will count against you in regard to your credit score.

So, let's break them down a little and look at what's on your credit report.

These are the worst things you can have, judgments and tax liens against you. Any of these will make a big dent in your credit score and they will continue to work against you for a very long time (up to 7 years). You don't want these if you can help it.

The next thing is your credit items. These are credit cards, loans, mortgages and any other credit account that you've had in the past. Most accounts that are considered old (closed more than 10 years ago) will not report unless you've had a collection filed for that account.

Every on-time payment will count in your

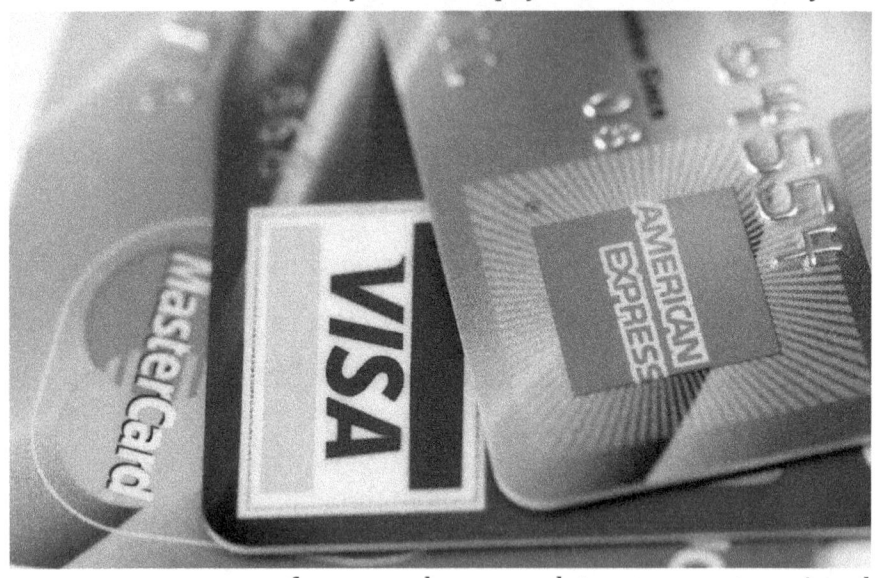

favor and every late payment, missed payment or collection will count against you. Each balance is reported as well and high balances will also count against you.

Remember we said before that you want to have a high available credit balance, but you also want to have a low balance on the credit you're using. What the credit reporting agency does is look at how much you're able to spend on all of your credit cards and add that together. That's your available credit balance. They then look at how much money you owe on each of those cards and add that all together.

The amount owed is divided by the amount available and that's your total balance percentage. You want to keep this percentage low because that reflects well on your credit card. A high percentage will look bad and lower your credit score.

The total amount of accounts that you have as well as the types of accounts will count towards your score as well. You want to have a moderate number of accounts (more than 10) as long as you can keep them all current.

Finally, the number of inquiries that you have will affect your score. You want to cut down on the amount of inquiries that you have because everyone is a slight ding to your account. What these are is every time that you apply for credit. That's why you want to apply for credit infrequently and only if you're sure you will get it. Getting the credit will help improve your score more than it will hurt for the inquiry.

- You want to make sure of a few important things in regard to your credit report:
- Have several different accounts (10 or more)?
- Keep all accounts current
- Avoid public records
- Keep your available balance high
- Keep the balance in use low
- Don't apply for credit unless necessary
- Never apply for credit unless you're sure you'll be approved
- Dispute accounts that aren't correct
- Make payments on any past due accounts and pay off collections

By doing all of these things your credit score will increase over time. It will take some time and you will need to work at it, but you'll be able to bring your credit score back up. Once you're able to bring your score back up, you'll find it even easier to get out of debt and you'll start saving better as well. The reason your credit score will affect this is because your credit score has a lot to do with you getting approved for everything from credit cards to car loans to housing. It also has to do with the interest rates that you're given. Staying out of debt means you have more money to put away towards your savings. it's a win all the way around.

Credit Reporting Agencies

There are three fundamental consumer announcing agencies: Trans-Union, Equifax, and Experian (in the past known as T.R.W.). These three significant information agencies have a lock on the revealing credit industry and summarize more than 90 percent of the credit report information in the United States. Because every one of the three agencies is rivaling one another for a similar customer base, they are incredibly serious with each other and don't share information. The rivalry has driven these agencies to extend their districts. The agencies currently give Information to supporters all through the world. The agencies are benefit situated, with profits originating from the people and businesses who buy into them as their hotspot for consumer information. Remember that a consumer detailing organization is decided on the painstaking quality, practicality, and precision of the consumer information it assembles. The way that the agencies don't impart Information to each other is both a gift and a revile. For instance, one report shows every single great record; you are fit as a fiddle. However, if another report shows an awful record, you are in a difficult situation. Many businesses and organizations buy into more than one credit detailing office to abstain from making expensive mistakes in deciding an individual's credit value. As clarified, the agencies get businesses and organizations to buy into them by demonstrating that their credit reports and credit files are the most accurate and complete Information accessible on the consumer (you and me).

The best credit organization is the one that re-ports both negative and positive Information with practicality and precision. Businesses and organizations depend intensely upon the practicality and exactness of the Information when endeavoring to settle on a qualified choice concerning credit value. Credit agencies should report truthful Information concerning foundation information and consumer credit propensities. Since credit agencies start announcing your experience information and consumer credit propensities from your first credit understanding, it is essential to build up or restore a strong consumer establishment at a convenient time. However, setting up and restoring isn't constantly a simple task to embrace. Realizing where to turn and what to search for is critical to beginning on the correct foot. So you ask how would I build up or restore my's-self as a capable credit-utilizing consumer? How about we investigate only a couple of thoughts that can be useful to you as a dependable credit consumer.

Where Do Agencies Get Information?

There are a large number of credit agencies situated all through the United States. A credit organization's fundamental capacity is to accumulate Information on you and put that information into a report called a credit report or a consumer report. A credit report is an archive that contains an accurate record of a person's consumer credit payment history. The report is generated by the credit organization and is only one of the snippets of Information used by an outsider to decide a person's credit value. We should note here for the future that a credit report is different from a consumer file. A consumer file is an assortment of the entirety of the Information assembled on a person by a credit organization. Your credit report is a changeless piece of your consumer file. The Fair Credit Reporting Act is a bit of enactment that administers what credit agencies can and can't get to.

A credit report must bear on a consumer's credit value, credit standing, credit limit, character, general reputation, personal qualities, or method of living." So, by definition, credit agencies have a wide range from which they can accumulate Information on you. Remember that each

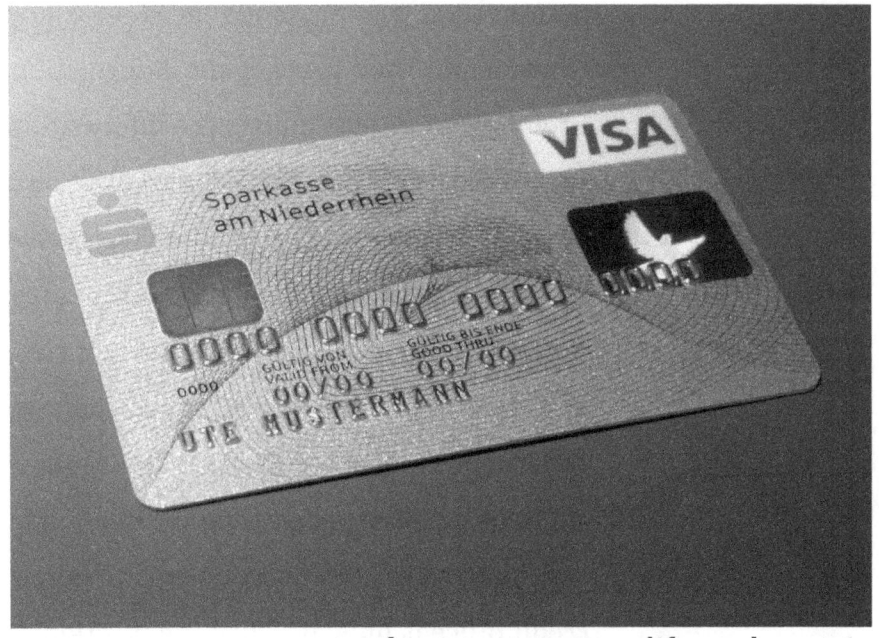

part of your consumer life and certain regions of your private life are available to the credit agencies. A case of the sort of Information a credit organization can put in your credit file and on your credit report is the act of composing terrible checks. The composition of an awful check thinks about your general reputation. If a business reports the composition of a terrible check to a credit office, the credit organization has the option to put that information in your consumer file and on your credit report. Since you recognize what kinds of Information the credit agencies can accumulate, you presently need to know from whom they can get the Information. Credit agencies accumulate the Information they need from businesses, organizations, open and private sources, and legislative workplaces. These are similar businesses, organizations, open and private sources, and legislative workplaces that you use consistently. The credit agencies request spots of business, promising complete and accurate credit information—this is how a credit office is judged. When the position of the business is joined with a credit organization, the two offer information about you that is crucial to the two. The entirety of the groups requested by the credit agencies depends upon the fulfillment and precision of the Information accumulated to help them in choices, including a person's credit value.

What's a Good Credit Score?

In the current economy, it's a lot harder to qualify for a loan. Presently you need an excellent credit score to qualify for most types of credit. So what's a good credit score rating?

850 is immaculate credit and the most elevated credit score rating conceivable; however, I've never personally observed anybody with an 850. A good credit score begins in the 670 territory. Scores lower than 670 are not viewed as good credit.

In general, credit score values range from 300 to 850. A lower value means that a person is less creditworthy, while a higher value means that he is more creditworthy. However, this interpretation is broadened by the lending companies using their respective financial data on their clients. Instead of referring to a high or a low credit score, they have developed certain brackets that explain how creditworthy a person is. The following explains what each range of credit scores mean:

- A credit score of 751 to 800 allows a borrower to apply for credit with the lowest interest rate and the most competitive amount because the lending companies have an assurance that he will not default in his monetary obligations. Many consider this score as the best. Someone who gets a score within this range can be almost certain their application will be granted.

- A credit score of 711 to 750 allows a borrower to apply for credit at competitive interest rates. While the person's credit standing is relatively good, a slightly higher interest rate would be charged to them compared to someone who scores 751 and up. Someone who scores at this range gets a relatively good credit standing.

- A credit score of 651 to 710 allows a borrower to apply for credit at moderate interest rates. This is the normal score that applicants must get to ensure that their application will be granted.

- A credit score of 581-650 may be allowed to apply for credit, but he must obtain it at high interest rates. This is because at this range, the possibility of risks and loses is getting high.
- A credit score of 300-580 does not allow a person to apply for credit. Their application may be granted, but they can only avail it if they are willing to pay the highest interest rate. This is because at this range, possibility of losses is very high.

However, one must take note that there is no general method in determining the credit score of a person. Its computation depends on the company assessing him. His credit score may be different when assessed by different companies, but also the range of scores may be interpreted to mean the same thing because of the elements considered in assessing him.

For instance, his score may be 375 in one company and 340 in another, but both scores mean that he is less creditworthy and has to repair his credit score fast.

Conclusion

After reading this plan you have to come up with a financial plan which will help you start to pay off your credit cards strategically. You then have to make sure that, no matter what, you follow this plan. Even if you find yourself in an emergency after a few months when your car breaks down, you should find another way to come up with your emergency funding. It is important that you continue to make more than the minimum payment on time with all your credit cards. The fewer fees you need to add into your balance, the quicker you will be able to pay off your credit card debt.

Another way to bring down credit card debt quickly, especially if you are overdrawn and missed a few payments, is to contact the credit card company. While many people don't realize this, most credit card companies want to work with you. The number one reason for this is they want to keep you as a customer, basically, so they can continue receiving your money. One strategy to use is to call and say that you would like to close your account. They will then try to focus on keeping your account open, which usually results in them dropping a few missed payment or over the limit fees. Another strategy to use is simply to explain to them what happened, why you were late, and tell them that you want to put your account in good standing. They are usually willing to drop some fees or so much money if you are willing to pay a certain amount off that day.

Don't hesitate, put all the notions of the book into practice immediately and improve your credit score!

Credit Secret Pratical

A Practical Guide, With All The Secrets And Tricks To Improve Your Credit Score; The Book That Will Change Your Credit Score Forever

John Cash – Credit Score Academy

INTRODUCTION **83**

LOOPHOLE TO RAISE YOUR CREDIT. **86**

How to Boost your Credit Score of Points 86

QUICK TIPS FOR REPAIRING YOUR CREDIT **91**

BECOME AN AUTHORIZED USER **95**

The Loophole They Don't Tell You About 101
How many credit cards do I need? 103
How To Get A Credit Card? 104
Have a good credit history: 105
Have an Aval: 106

THE RIGHT WAY TO CHECK YOUR CREDIT REPORT **108**

All you need to know about credit reports 108
What Is Present in a Credit Report? 109
Personal Information 110
Public Records 110
Accounts 111
Credit Inquiries 112
How to Fix Errors in Credit Report? 114
Some other errors that happen in a credit report are as follows – 120
Who Can Check Your Credit Report? 125

HOW TO OBTAIN A GOOD CREDIT SCORE: **129**

Amount Owed accounts for 30 Percent of your credit score. 132
The Length of Credit History counts for 15% of your credit score. 134
Amount of New Credit accounts for 10 Percent of your credit score 137
Kind of Credit Utilized accounts for 10% of your credit score. 138

HOW TO USE AND FIX IDENTITY THEFT **141**

What to Do If You Are a Victim of Identity Theft 141
Contact your Bank Agency 150
Try and Avoid the Collection Agency 152
Apply for a Secured Credit Card 154
Consider a Company that Specializes in Credit Repair 155

THE RIGHT MINDSET **158**

Using Consolidation or Settlement Strategies to Pay Down Debts 159
Negotiate with Credit Companies 160
Cut the Credit Cards 161
Talking to Creditors 162

CREDIT COUNSELING..162
DEBT MANAGEMENT PLAN 163
DEBT SETTLEMENT PROGRAM 163
GOODWILL LETTERS 165

YOUR FINANCIAL FREEDOM...168

WHAT DOES FINANCIAL FREEDOM MEAN? 169
CREDIT CARDS AND FINANCIAL FREEDOM—IS IT SAFE?.....................170
THE BEST HABITS TO HELP YOU REACH AND PROTECT YOUR FINANCIAL FREEDOM 171
MAKE A BUDGET 172
SET UP AN AUTOMATIC SAVINGS ACCOUNT..173
KEEP YOUR CREDIT IN MIND WITHOUT OBSESSING OVER IT..............174
IT IS FINE TO LIVE BELOW YOUR MEANS...175
SPEAK WITH A FINANCIAL ADVISOR 176
COMPLETELY PAY OFF YOUR CREDIT CARDS 177
TRACK YOUR SPENDING 178
CONTINUE YOUR EDUCATION...179
MAKE SURE YOU WRITE DOWN WHAT FINANCIAL FREEDOM MEANS TO YOU 180
THE BEST HABITS TO HELP YOU REACH AND PROTECT YOUR FINANCIAL FREEDOM 182

THE 5 BEST WAYS TO PAY OFF DEBTS 193

CREDIT CARD DEBT IS THE COSTLIEST DEBT.....................................194
DEBT MANAGEMENT TIPS 196
WHAT'S THE BEST APPROACH TO DEAL WITH HUGE CREDIT CARD DEBT?............197
IF YOU NEED TO MANAGE YOUR CREDIT CARD APRS 199
SETTLING YOUR OWN DEBTS..202

CREDIT SCORE MYTHS TO UNLEARN 207

CLOSING CREDIT ACCOUNTS WILL HELP YOUR SCORE.........................209
YOU CAN INCREASE YOUR SCORE BY ASKING YOUR CREDIT CARD COMPANY TO LOWER YOUR LIMITS 211
YOU NEED TO PAY INTEREST TO OBTAIN A GOOD CREDIT SCORE.........212
YOUR CLOSED ACCOUNTS SHOULD INDICATE "CLOSED BY CONSUMER," OR THEY WILL HURT YOUR SCORE...214
CREDIT COUNSELING IS WAY WORSE THAN BANKRUPTCY...................215
WHEN YOU CLOSE YOUR MANY CREDIT ACCOUNTS, YOUR CREDIT SCORE WILL IMPROVE 216
ONE THING THAT AFFECTS YOUR SCORE IS THE AMOUNT OF MONEY YOU MAKE...218
CREDIT SCORES TEND TO CHANGE ONLY A FEW TIMES A YEAR.........219
ONCE YOU HAVE A BAD CREDIT SCORE, IT IS IMPOSSIBLE TO GET LOANS OR CREDITS 220
YOU CAN HAVE AN EXCELLENT CREDIT REPORT IF YOU HAVE NO CREDIT 221
BRINGING A BALANCE TO YOUR CREDIT CARD ALSO HELPS YOUR SCORE.............222
YOU CAN'T RECOVER FROM A BAD CREDIT SCORE. IT STAYS WITH YOU FOR LIFE..223

BREAKDOWN OF THE CREDIT STAGES AND PHASES **226**

KNOW HOW MUCH CREDIT YOU NEED 227
START SMALL 229
PROTECT WHAT YOU HAVE 231
THERE ARE SEVERAL WAYS TO DO THIS 232
YOU'RE IN IT FOR THE LONG HAUL 233

CONCLUSION **236**

Introduction

The reality is that we live in a society that almost demands that we have some form of credit, not to get ahead, but simply to survive. When we are without it, we suffer in more ways than one.

What better reason is there to start mending our financial health than this? Yes, it can be scary, unpredictable, and stressful but by applying the strategies outlined in this book, you can find your way to a successful credit repair without the additional expense of hiring services to do it for you.

There is an excellent benefit to fixing your credit yourself. Not only do you save yourself from an additional expense when you are already financially strapped, but you become an expert and play a major starring role in your own life.

By applying the information in this book, you will have enough resources at your disposal to get your finances back on track. They say that it takes three weeks for you to get into long-lasting habits. When you are able to budget and watch how you spend, you will quickly find yourself developing new habits.

This guidebook will cover all of the tips and tricks that you need to know in order to get to know about credit scores. You can utilize these administrations if you are worried about wholesale fraud, or when you are building your credit profile and you have to screen your advancement. If your requirement for a credit card score is easygoing, you don't have to leave behind month-to-month expenses to pay for an observing help.

loophole to raise your credit.

How to Boost your Credit Score of Points

You can in any case improve your FICO rating regardless of whether you can't get any negative things expelled, or on the off chance that you choose to sit tight for them to tumble off of your report normally. It's likewise imperative to deal with accumulations with consideration so you don't erroneously reset the date of the legal time limit.

Pursue these means as a major aspect of your far-reaching credit fix system to ensure you make the most all things considered and dodge accidental difficulties that could cause enduring harm.

Survey Your Accounts in Collections

Start off by taking a gander at your ongoing accumulations. They have the most effect on your credit on the grounds that more up to date obligation is weighted all the more vigorously. Additionally, focus on the sort of obligation you're paying.

Medicinal obligation doesn't influence you acknowledge as much as different sorts of obligation so center around any non-therapeutic obligation first. Attempt to make full installments since halfway installments can reset as far as possible for to what extent those records can stay on your credit report.

You can likewise attempt to arrange a settlement with the accumulation organization to pay short of what you owe. Simply understand that you may need to report the sum that was rejected as pay on your assessment form, which could bring about higher expenses and even a higher duty rate on the off chance that it knocks you into another level of pay.

Another issue with satisfying delinquent payment accumulations can happen if the gathering office goes about as though you haven't made any installment whatsoever. Maintain a strategic distance from this trick by getting installment understandings recorded as a hard copy and keeping duplicates of all reports identified with the record.

Keep on checking Your Credit

When you've dealt with your records in accumulations, ensure those progressions are precisely thought about your credit report. It might take a month or two for the records to drop off, so hold up a little while before checking your report and your FICO rating.

In the event that you don't perceive any positive changes, or the negative thing is as yet recorded, you should document a debate with the credit authority. For whatever length of time that you kept great records, you ought to have all the fitting documentation your requirement for a snappy debate process.

Quick Tips for Repairing Your Credit

Getting negative things erased from your credit report can have emotional outcomes on your financial assessment, however it's a procedure that can take a ton of time.

In case you're searching for fast upgrades, there are as yet a couple of techniques you can utilize. Some are little fixes while others can at present have a major effect, so check the entire rundown to see which ones you can attempt today to fix your credit.

Lower Your Credit Utilization Ratio

The closer you are to maximizing your cards, the lower your FICO rating will be.

In this way, it bodes well that squaring away your equalizations on your charge cards can bring down your proportion and increment your score. Concentrate on maximized cards as opposed to those with low adjusts; thusly, you could see as much as a 100-point increment over a time of a couple of months.

Request a Credit Limit Increase on Credit Cards

On the off chance that you can't bear to satisfy additional obligation to diminish your credit usage, regardless you get an opportunity for enhancements. Call at least one of your charge card backers and solicitation an expansion on your card limit. You would prefer not to really charge anything else than you as of now owe, you essentially need to have a higher farthest point with the goal that your current parity comprises of a littler level of your accessible credit.

Here's a model. Let's assume you owe $5,000 on a card with a $10,000 limit. You'd use half of your credit. Yet, in the event that you got your limit up to $15,000, at that point your $5,000 equalization would just use 33% of your breaking point.

When deciding to your loan boss, it helps on the off chance that you've submitted normal on-time installments since your commencement with them. More than likely, they'll esteem client faithfulness enough to enable your credit to line.

Become an Authorized User

Building your record as a consumer takes a great deal of time, however there is an alternate way accessible. Locate a dear companion or relative who has long-standing, solid credit and request to turn into an approved client on at least one of their records. That Mastercard record will naturally be added surprisingly report completely.

There's a touch of hazard associated with this move: if your companion or relative quits making installments or conveys an enormous equalization, those negative passages will be added surprisingly history. In like manner, in the event that you rack up additional adjusts and don't help make any installments you're in charge of, the other individual's credit will wind up harmed. This can be an incredible strategy, yet it requires some alert.

Solidify Your Credit Card Debt

Another fast method to fix your credit is to consider getting an obligation solidification advance. It's essentially a kind of close to home advance that you utilize the result your different Mastercards, at that point pay a solitary month to month balance on the advance.

Contingent upon your financing costs, you may have the option to get a good deal on your regularly scheduled installments by getting a lower advance rate. Shop around utilizing pre-endorsements to perceive what sort of rates you meet all requirements for and how they stack up contrasted with your present card rates.

Regardless of whether you make back the initial investment on your regularly scheduled installments, your FICO assessment will at present observe a lift since portion advances are seen more positively than spinning credit.

Get a Credit-developer Loan

Littler banks and credit associations regularly offer credit-manufacturer advances to enable people to fix their credit. When you take out the credit, the assets are stored into a record that you're not ready to get to.

You at that point start making regularly scheduled installments on the advance sum. When you've reimbursed the whole credit, the assets are discharged for you to utilize.

It might appear to be unusual to profit you can't spend, however it's a path for the monetary establishment to feel ensured while you get an opportunity to substantiate yourself as a capable borrower.

When you effectively complete your installments and get the cash, the bank reports your installments as on-time to the credit authorities to assist your FICO rating.

Utilize just a little segment of your credit limit

"Credit use" is credit-represent the level of your credit breaking point you're utilizing. The sum you utilize powerfully affects your FICO assessment — just paying on time matters more.

Most specialists prescribe going no higher than 30% on any card, and lower is better for your score. When your Mastercard backer reports a lower equalization to the credit departments, your score can profit. Your score won't be harmed by past high credit usage once you've cut adjusts down.

Get a co-signer

In case you're experiencing considerable difficulties gaining admittance to credit, ask a relative or companion to co-sign an advance or charge card. This is a colossal support: You're requesting that this individual put their credit notoriety on hold for you and to assume full liability for reimbursement in the event that you don't pay as concurred. The co-underwriter may likewise be turned down on the off chance that they apply for more credit later in light of the fact that this record will be considered in surveying their money related profile. Utilize this alternative with alert and be sure you can reimburse. Inability to do so can harm the co-endorser's credit notoriety and your relationship.

Pay on schedule

Take care of your tabs and any current credit extensions on schedule, without fail. No single factor influences your financial assessment as much as your history of on-time installments. When you are reconstructing credit, you can't bear to miss an installment.

Late installments remain on your credit answers for as long as seven years, so these take more time to recoup from than some other credit slips up.

On the off chance that a few bills have just become delinquent, however, organize the ones where your record is as yet open. Gatherers may make the most clamor, yet they aren't your top need.

The Loophole They Don't Tell You About

To begin with, understand that all credit reporting is done in real time, *electronically* in digital format. There is no paperwork involved whatsoever. And this is your key to win the war, *on the big three.* And you are now going to learn why and how you can win.

Turns out, that all your financial accounts and credit checks, from banks to cards to applications alike, *are digitally reported.* There are *never* any wet signed documents of verification regarding your credit reporting.

Each month all your creditors, from banks to credit card companies, send electronic files which all contain the transaction details of your accounts to each of the big three CRA's. These Credit Bureaus as they are also known as, then place your information into your personal credit report *without-any-legal-verification. none!*

What's worse is that no one else is even verifying as to whether or not these accounts are actually **your** accounts. There is no one checking as to *if* this credit data reporting *being sent digitally each month* is even correct. There are no paper trails or paper records other than what is sent digitally to verify what the creditors or bank reports in order to *make certain* that they are reporting the correct information. *Ever.*

This is the *loophole* that can change it all for you too. It's a wonder why only a handful of us know.

Without Signed and Documented Verification, neither *Equifax, Experian nor Transunion* know for certain **if** *what* the banks and credit card companies are reporting each month to them, are correct.

Albeit they can be correct, but the fact remains, that no one is verifying, and no one is certain. No one outside of your own beliefs knows for sure. This fact alone can give you the power to crush that low score, once and for all, and *turn it all around today.*

The *FCRA* is now the rule maker and law writer for the *Big Three CRA's.* And as good fortune would have it, the FCRA laws, like all laws do, will protect your rights as a citizen of the good old USA.

How many credit cards do i need?

There are several types of credit cards, starting with the world's leading payment brands, as they are:

- Visa
- Mastercard
- American Express
- Diners Club

And also, according to the category of credit card you acquire, according to your monthly income, the most common are:

- Classic
- Gold
- Platinum
- Signature
- Infinite

But as demand for these cards grew, each leading payment brand created new versions of these card categories, being unique and with different features and benefits.

How To Get A Credit Card?

Some financial institutions require that the person who wishes to acquire a credit card have a passive account with them, that is, a savings account, salary account or a fixed-term deposit. It is worth mentioning that this is not a requirement, but it helps the financial institution to have prior knowledge of your income and can facilitate the acquisition of a card. The requirements to be able to obtain one, are depending on what is requested by the bank, but next the most essential will be announced.

You must show that you generate monthly income and that you do not exceed your capacity for over-indebtedness. You can attach your pay stubs, receipts for fees or other means to support your economy. The more years they have worked in a company, the lower the risk for the bank, which helps in the credit evaluation.

Have a good credit history:

If you are a person who has had a credit card before and has been late in their payments for about 4 to 6 months, let me tell you, you do not have a good credit history and it will be very complicated to get a credit card, because of the risk that represents. But if you are a person who is just beginning with the banking and getting his first card, in good time, you have the proper tips to avoid being reported in the central risk.

Have an Aval:

If you are with a bad category in the central risk, but you paid all your debt with that financial institution and the system is still not updated. You may be asked for a guarantee and your letter of no debt, as collateral for the loan to be given.

These are only some of the requirements that banks request, however it will depend on the credit evaluation that they make, analyzing many more points

The right way to check your credit report

All you need to know about credit reports

Every credit bureau collects a lot of information about you, and all of that is included in your credit report. If someone wants to know about your credit usage in all these years, then one look at the credit report would reveal everything. The report has everything starting from whether you have cleared all your bills on time to the amount of debt that you might owe. The three credit bureaus, that is, Equifax, Experian, and Transunion, are the ones that collect that information and compile them in the form of a report. All the information included in your report is collected from different sources (that is, lenders).

Whenever you want to apply for any type of loan or credit like student loans, credit cards, mortgage loans, and auto loans, every lender would want to have a look at your credit report. They will be granting you the credit only after they have evaluated your credit report, and everything seems fine. Your stats should match the terms set by them and if not, then you will not be getting your favorable rates.

What Is Present in a Credit Report?

The information that is present in your credit report is utilized in finding out your credit score. And all that information will be used by lenders to predict what your future behavior with respect to credit is going to be. In this section, I am going to explain some of the information that you will find on a credit report –

Personal Information

This is the list of information that can be used in the future to identify you as a person. All of this information is not utilized to find your credit score. Some of the things that are included in this section are your name, any misspellings that have been brought to light by creditors, aliases (if any), home addresses (past and current), Social Security Number, employers (past and current) and phone numbers.

Public Records

If there have been any legal actions taken against the financial accounts of the person, then they will be listed under the public records section. But any non- financial information or misdemeanors or arrests are not included here. It is solely meant for financial, legal actions, and if you have any public record in your credit report, then that is considered to be bad and you are probably not going to receive credits or loans.

Accounts

Any installment loans or revolving credit are included in this section. There are three categories to these accounts – closed, negative, and open. When you have been on good terms with the creditor, they will report the same. Your accounts will be considered to be in a good position. But sometimes you might not find certain account information because it was not reported by the creditors. If your creditor has reported then monthly balances up two years on any account could be listed in this section.

Some of the negative things that can be included are bankruptcies, late payments, or any type of account that has been forwarded to the collection or may be charged off. If an account has been transferred or settled, then that might not have any bad impact on your score or report. It would definitely be something that any creditor would look more closely at.

Credit Inquiries

Another section that your credit report is that of the credit inquiries where the names of those businesses will be listed who had recently inquired about your credit information. Usually, your credit report might have an inquiry up till two years from when it was made.

Some things that are not mentioned in your credit report are your marital information, your education level, or even your bank balance. If a creditor has reported the name of your spouse, then that might be included in a report. But if you have had a divorce and you do not want the name of your spouse on the credit report, then you can proceed with disputing the information displayed on your credit report.

How to Fix Errors in Credit Report?

Mistakes are made by everyone, but if the mistake is too vital and it is going to affect your credit score negatively, then you should not put up with it. The CFPB or Consumer Financial Protection Bureau has stated that the main complaint they receive is how the credit reports contain incorrect information. The FTC or the Federal Trade Commission had conducted a study in which it was found that 26% of the participants brought to light that their reports had at least one error because of which their creditworthiness was reduced. So, these catastrophic errors are what going to prevent you from getting competitive interest rates, favorable lending terms, and a new line of credits. And this is also why you should keep checking your credit report to ensure that there are no errors in it. But to make matters easier, before we move on to how you can fix the error, I am going to provide you with an overview of the common mistakes that are found in a report.

Sometimes people keep changing their names while applying for credit, and in that case, if an error occurs then that is because of you. So, you should always be using the same name when you are applying for credit and be consistent with it everywhere. Even if you are using initials, they should remain the same as well. If you do not do that, then it might happen that your report is overlapped with someone else who has the same name as you. And the same consistency should be maintained with things like your address and Social Security number.

This was one type of mistake. Another type of mistake is when you failed to enter all the details in your credit report. This is when a person is often denied credit because there was no credit file, or there was an insufficient credit file. In these cases, all the credit accounts belonging to a person are not often included in their credit file and that is when the problem arises. But you should also keep in mind that several all-purpose credit cards issued by banks and national department store credit cards are not included in the credit report and not every creditor will give the information to the credit bureaus voluntarily. This is mainly because creditors are not really required to do that.

So, if you find that your credit report does not have some information or account, you have to first talk to your creditor and tell them that they have to report to the credit bureaus. If they don't agree with it, then you should consider the option of moving your account to some other credit bureau who will report these things regularly.

Some other errors that happen in a credit report are as follows

There has been a clerical error in entering the information, for example, your address or name, especially when you had submitted a hand-written application.

Sometimes it might also happen that someone else's loan or credit card payments have been assigned to your account.

In case you decide to close your loan or credit card account, you have to make sure that it is stated 'closed by the grantor'; otherwise, it might give the wrong notion that it was not you but the creditor who closed your account.

Lenders might be seeing double when the same account has been reported twice, which might give the idea that your debt is actually higher than it appears to be, or you have more open lines of credit.

In case you have undergone a divorce, then your credit report should not include any debts that belonged to your former spouse.

If there are any bad debts or mysterious accounts, then it might also be because of identity thieves and you should be careful about that because there are people who are simply waiting to get your personal information.

Also, if seven years have already passed after a bad debt, then it is the duty of the credit- reporting company to remove it. If it has not yet been removed, then you have to report it otherwise your score will be unnecessarily affected.

Now that you know about the common errors that can happen in your credit report, let us discuss how you can remove them. Firstly, you should contact both the organization and the bureau if you want a quick resolution to your problem. Any incomplete or inaccurate information on your credit report is the responsibility of both parties. And this has been stated under the Fair Credit Reporting Act. Also, all three credit bureaus have their online mode of dispute submission, so the process becomes even easier.

So, you have to start by stating the information that has not been provided correctly in your credit report. Until and unless the bureaus consider the dispute to be false, they are under obligation to investigate your claims within thirty days. In order to make your case strong and provide all the support, you should add copies of documents but never provide the originals. Your complete address and name should be correctly mentioned, and you should also state all facts clearly with proper reasons. And in the end, you should mention whether you want correction or deletion. Also, to make it a better application, you should include one copy of your report and then circle all those things that you want to change. The way you communicate can place a very big impact and so, you have to be crystal clear.

If you are going to mail your letter, then send it only to a mail that is certified and also request the return receipt. In this way, no one can disbelieve your claim of the credit bureau receiving your application. Also, you must keep a copy of everything that you have enclosed along with a dispute letter.

The next step that you must take is to write a letter to the appropriate information provider or creditor, mentioning everything about the dispute that you have raised. Here too, you have to include copies of everything. The entire process can take anywhere between thirty to ninety days. Moreover, there are certain states that will even provide you a free credit report so that you can verify the information on the updated report and know that everything is correct. To know whether you qualify for this service or not, you have to contact the credit bureau.

Who Can Check Your Credit Report?

If you think that your entire credit history is available to anyone who wishes to access it and all they have to do is search it on Google, then you are wrong. Your financial information is quite secure, and it can be accessed by only those who have a legitimate reason to see it.

There are several organizations who might want to check your credit report, and some of them have been mentioned below –

Banks – Banks might have the need to check whether you are creditworthy or not. Especially if you want to open a new account and this will remain the same even if there is no credit card linked to your account. This is because if someone is not creditworthy, there will be higher chances of that person to abandon or overdraw their accounts. Also, many people don't know that overdraft protection is a type of line of credit and so applying for that would also lead to the banks pulling out your credit report.

Creditors – Any potential or current creditor has the right to pull out your credit report so that they can determine whether you are creditworthy or not. Both the terms and approval of a loan or credit card depend on your creditworthiness.

Utility Companies – The utility company can ask for your credit report if you are opening a new connection or opting for a cellphone service with them. There are certain states where a bad credit might lead to the utility companies denying you any service.

Student Loan Providers – If PLUS loans have been applied for, then before granting such loans, the creditworthiness of the parents is checked. Your credit report might be pulled if you are applying for any type of private loan that is not included in the federal government. Also, you won't be allowed to apply for a new federal loan if you already have on open.

Insurance Companies – Your insurance scores based on your credit are required to find out your insurance rates.

Employers – There are certain states where the employers have the right to pull out your credit report. These reports will not include your date of birth or even your account numbers.

Landlords – Landlords might pull out your credit report to see whether you have the habit of clearing payments timely. The better your credit, the more easily you will get a home/apartment on rent because they assume that the rent will be cleared timely.

How to obtain a good credit score:

There are five criteria that your credit is scored upon which are rather simple to follow. Your Payment History accounts for 35% of your credit score. Do you pay your bills on time? If you don't do anything else yet make timely payments, you will have a good credit score in two years. Staying away from late payments is one of the most effective ways to support your credit. Otherwise your past actions will continue to harm your credit score. One ongoing multi day late payment will bring down your credit score, in all probability by 20! A few late payments and your score will drop extremely far, exceptionally fast. Being late by multiple days can hurt your score considerably more, and they are a main problem when assessing your credit score. Know that the later the wrongdoing, the more negative the impact on your score. While there is often a grace period, anything over 30 days will cause real damage to your credit score. Make sure to analyze your debt and check in with your bank statements. Be very diligent in making timely payments and deal with accounts before they are late or go to assortment. Try not to overextend yourself so that it harms your odds of making timely payments. If you have old late payments that can't be removed or fixed from your credit report, realize that time heals old injuries, and your score will increase if no new misconducts are reported. Always remember to pay before the "Grace Period" placed on your credit cards. Creditors charge extra expenses for late payments. This is an exceptionally enormous benefit for the banks. A bank may charge a $30-$35 expense for being 2 hours late on your payments! (be sure to look at the fine print on everything) Numerous banks have also introduced other feeds associated with multi-day late payments triggered even before the 30 days. Don't cut it too close with your due date. Get your payments in fast or set up automatic payments so you don't forget.

Amount Owed accounts for 30 Percent of your credit score.

The credit scoring model determines credit balance, usually against your high credit limit. This is calculated in rates. It's imperative to keep your balances as low as could be allowed. If you have a card with a $5,000 credit limit, keeping your balance beneath $500 places you in the 10% scope of accessible credit. There are thresholds in debt proportion that will make your credit score bounce higher. These thresholds are 70%, half, 30% and 10%. If you can't pay off your credit cards for the whole amount, pay them down BELOW the following conceivable edge. Calculate your credit limits along these lines. If you have a card with a $5,000 limit, increase 5000 x.10 (or.30,.50,.70) You will need to pay your balance for at least under these sums. For this situation - under $500 (or $1500, $2500 or $3500).

Keep in mind; the priipal activity is to check your credit report for credit limits. If your high limit isn't reporting, the scoring model will utilize your balance as your credit limit. This implies you're utilizing 100% of your availability. Call your creditor and make sure they correct it. Conveyance of debt is a simple method to make sure you keep up a solid score.

Try to have a good spread of debt with a lower balance to limit proportion. For instance, it's better to have $2,000 debt on 5 cards than to have $10,000 on a card with all others paid off. In the case you're creeping up towards your credit limits, apply for more credit, or request an increase in credit from your current accounts.

This criterion depends on all out availability, not estimate of availability. It doesn't make a difference if you need $500 or $50,000. It's how you handle it that matters. Breaking debt onto extra cards or credit lines can assist you with raising your score rapidly.

The Length of Credit History counts for 15% of your credit score.

Length of credit history is about time the length or period you've had your credit accounts. If you've had a credit record open for 15 years, it is more stable than if you have had one for just two months. An important hint here is never to close your credit cards. Keep your old accounts open if they are in good standing, regardless of whether you don't utilize them and there's a zero balance. However, keep in mind that you need to use your credit lines a little to keep the active. Accounts unused for over 6 months become idle and are overlooked by the credit bureaus, except if there is a reprobate action joined to that record. Keeping your credit lines open likewise helps in improving your credit availability, clarified in the previous section. If you want to include credit, ask your card organization to increase your credit limit. The best way to increase your credit lines, beside getting another card, is to broaden your line on an old record with a good and long history. Be sure they report the credit amount increment to the bureaus accurately. A standard factor of amazingly good credit scores are long credit narratives. Credit reports that possess old accounts with a fifteen to twenty-year history will probably have a lot higher scores. In conclusion, it is important to add older stable credit lines to your report and keep them in good standing even when not using them.

Amount of New Credit accounts for 10 Percent of your credit score

New credit means fresh out of the box or newly opened accounts. If you have just opened your account you will need to build up its authority gradually. If you have recently applied for 10 credit cards, banks will, in general, accept the likelihood that possibly you've lost your employment and are needing a backup plan. Try to begin with one little credit extension and work from that point. Every time you start a new credit line, make sure that you can deal with the payments reliably, not be late, and keep your balances as low as is allowed, or paid off.

Kind of Credit Utilized accounts for 10% of your credit score.

The credit scoring model loves to see that you have an assortment of credit types in your file. The absolute best arrangement of credit is to have a home loan, a vehicle payment and a couple of credit cards. This credit is spread crosswise over various types of lenders and sort of credit reached out to you. There are a couple of types of credit to avoid. Payday loans are terrible to have credit with and your scores will likely be damaged for having these types of high-risk loans. Other very awful types of credit are the offers that enable you to have no payments for a year. These are hazardous, because the conditions of the understanding usually incorporate that if you don't pay the loan off in a year, on day 366 you will owe the whole years' worth of payments at normally 20% interest. This is a debacle already in the works. Individuals who more than once go for these offers are individuals who fall into credit difficulty. You ought not have that sort of credit on your credit report.

How to use and fix identity theft

What to Do If You Are a Victim of Identity Theft

Have you ever seen this happen? You just received a collection notice in the mail for an account you didn't use or even know about, you received a credit card in the mail you never wanted or opened, or you were simply turned down for a loan or credit card due to a low FICO score with accounts that weren't even yours. If there has been one of these cases, you are most likely a victim of identity theft.

You might feel robbed, betrayed and left wondering how this might happen to you. Your credit scores were most likely impacted negatively. You may need a loan or credit, and this condition prohibits you from receiving it. To fix the damage that has already happened and to mitigate potential future harm, you need to take control and figure out what to do next.

Criminal laws regulate identity theft. According to the Identity Theft and Assumption Deterrence Act of 1998, it is a felony to "consciously pass or use, without legal authority, a means of identifying another person with the intention of committing, or aiding or abetting, any criminal conduct that constitutes a breach of Federal law or that constitutes a crime under any State or local statute applicable." The law is in place to provide offenders with a consolidated complaint process, as well as improve the criminal laws surrounding identity theft. If you're a victim of identity theft, prompt action is required. The law allows claimants to challenge unauthorized charges; however, there are some time-limits that need to be followed.

Notify the creditor. When you find unauthorized charges on your credit or debit card, then you were most likely a victim of identity theft. The good news is that the Equal Credit Billing Act limits any responsibility for unauthorized charges to $50. When you discover the unauthorized charges, you will have to write down your trustee, disputing the questionable payments.

Write the letter of disagreement to the agency "Billing inquiries" of your creditor. Make sure you send the certified letter to your trustee and you know it's hitting you. Notify the creditor as soon as the unwanted payment is identified and make sure that your letter hits them within 60 days of the first bill revealing the mistake. Keep yourself a copy of the letter. Under statute, the creditor must respond within 30 days of receiving the message, and the conflict must be settled within two billing cycles.

Notify your bank. If your debit card has been stolen, you will report it to your bank within two working days. Under the Electronic Fund Transfer Act, you will only be held liable for $50 in unauthorized charges; however, you will be responsible for $500 of unauthorized charges if you report the unauthorized charges between three and 60 days. Unless you wait until 60 days later, you can lose all of the money stolen from your account. If your debit card has a Visa or MasterCard mark, both firms will limit your liabilities to $50 per card in unauthorized charges.

It's better that you alert your suppliers and banks as soon as you can or your debit cards, credit cards and even personal checks have been stolen if you detect fraudulent charges. The longer you wait to contact the lender, the greater the chance that some or all of the unauthorized charges will be placed on you.

Fraud alert. If you've been a victim of identity theft, it's important to create a warning about fraud. If you call credit reporting agencies, you will have to choose between two different types of fraud alerts-the expanded warning and the original notice.

The expanded notice entitles you to receive two free credit reports from each credit reporting agency per year; however, for seven years, the fraud alert must stay on your register. The most common type of warning against fraud is the original alarm. This will live 90 days on your file and will send you one free credit report from each of the three reporting agencies.

You must have a police report and evidence of the theft or attempted fraud to create an extended warning. You may request that for your protection, only the last four digits of your Social Security number appear on your credit report. You may also cancel any warning about fraud at any time.

To set up a fraud alert for your own protection is in your best interest. This means the robber can't open credit in your name. You will notify the other credit reporting offices whether you call one of the credit reporting agencies to set up the fraud alert.

Your credit report and credit score are important to you and to your future earnings. Make sure you check them regularly to ensure you're not a victim of identity theft.

Police report. If you suspect that you are a victim of identity theft, it is in your best interests to lodge a police report. Some creditors may require that a police report be used as evidence of the incident. Many police stations hesitate to take a call on identity theft. Assure your submission is permanent. Make sure that you have a copy of the report for your history, because credit card companies and banks may need to see the report and search for unauthorized charges. Remember, make sure that you have the name and phone number of the prosecutor, in case the investors need to talk to him or her.

Social Security Administration. If your Social Security card has been stolen or you know your Social Security number has been used to open new accounts, you will call the Department of Social Security. They will most of the time issue you a new Social Security number and card. To apply for a new Social Security number, you must provide evidence that someone using your account is still harming you. Your sex, U.S. residency, or legal immigration status, and name will need to be confirmed.

Postal inspector. When you believe that your mail was robbed or sent to a different location, you were most likely a victim of identity theft in which a criminal rummaged through your mail or used a Change of Address form to give them your mail. Contact the postal inspector for documentation and prosecute this fraud.

Department of Motor Vehicles. If you have stolen your driver's license, you need to contact your state agency that issued your license. Most of the time, you can locate their contact information by checking the Department of Motor Vehicles in your state online. They will cancel your license and give you instructions on how to get another license.

Federal Trade Commission. You will report the crime to the Federal Trade Commission (FTC) if you've been a victim of identity theft. Call them at IDTHEFT (877), or at www.idtheft.gov. Although the FTC does not prosecute identity theft, it exchanges concerns with local regulatory bodies that support the federal fight against identity theft.

Contact your Bank Agency

Once you went over your credit report and determined that everything is correct, the next step in repairing your credit history is to contact creditors with whom you have delinquent accounts. You should repair these accounts as soon as possible to successfully repair your credit.

In many cases, the creditor's priority is to recover as much of the account receivable as possible. Many people are surprised at how accommodating they can be in terms of organizing a payment process: in many cases, the creditor will eliminate interest or even reduce the bill and return it for immediate payment. If you can't pay immediately, propose a payment plan for the creditor that you can stick to: Creditors will accommodate most payment proposals because, again, your primary interest will be to recover the debt.

Remember that the reason you're doing this is to repair your credit history, so under no circumstances should you commit to a payment plan with your creditors that you won't be able to meet would only end up making problems worse in the future. If a creditor has repeated problems with a client, it is unlikely that there is much trust in the relationship, so they probably won't want to help you. Instead, choose something you can meet and explain your current financial situation to the creditor. By doing this, you can often achieve credit repair fairly quickly.

Try and Avoid the Collection Agency

The worst and last step a creditor will take is to sell your outstanding debt to a collection agency. In terms of credit repair, this is basically the worst thing that can happen because it means that whoever you owed money to consider your chances of recovering it so low that you are willing to lose some of the debt. In most cases, the creditor sells the debt to the collection agency at a large discount, often half the amount owed.

When a debtor sold his loan to a collection agency, he just "canceled" it and created the lowest possible mark on his credit history. If this happens, try and act as soon as possible after being contacted by the collection agent. Before you negotiate with the collection company, talk to your creditor. See if the creditor will remove the "canceled" mark from your credit history. This is something they will do sometimes, in exchange for an immediate payment.

If your creditor is not interested in negotiating payment, you would be in trouble with the collection agent. It can and will happen that the debt collector stays in a very intimidating and threatening position, usually implying that they are willing to take you to trial. The two points to keep in mind is that the collection company bought your debt for less than the amount owed, and you are unlikely to be sued. Your best solution is to offer to make an immediate payment for less than the actual balance of your debt. Most companies will accept this, usually because making a profit on any payment that exceeds 50% of their debt and offering to pay immediately allows them to close their file and work on other issues. When dealing with a collection agent, only offer full payment as a last resort.

Apply for a Secured Credit Card

Credit repair can be a slow process, and you may find yourself building a bit of credit backing slowly over a long period of time. A good place to start is with a "secured" credit card. These credit cards are issued by banking agencies that generally target people who have bad credit. Unlike a regular credit card, for which you will no doubt be rejected if you have a bad credit, it is a secured credit, the card usually requires you to give an initial deposit equivalent to the credit limit of the card. That is, you give the company $500 for a card with a credit limit of $500, and they reserve the right to use that deposit against any outstanding balance that remains for too long.

From the issuer's point of view, their bad credit won't matter because they don't take any risk: you'll never owe them more money than you've already given them to start with. From your point of view, secured cards are far from ideal, but if you have bad credit and need to participate in credit repair, you have no choice.

Once you have a secured credit card, use it sparingly but regularly and be sure to make all your payments on time. By doing this over a long period of time, you will slowly repair your credit history and regain the confidence of creditors who rejected you in the past.

Consider a Company that Specializes in Credit Repair

If you find that none of the above works for you in terms of credit repair, consider going to a company that specializes in this type of process. Many of these companies will offer to "clean up your credit record" for a fee. While the services of a credit repair company can be much more helpful, depending on your situation, you must be very careful to avoid scams and read all the fine print that is in most cases.

The basic strategy of most credit repair companies will be to encourage you to claim absolutely everything on your credit report with your credit bureau. The idea is to flood the office with more requests than they can respond to within 30 days, because remember that if the office can't provide documentation for something in your file within 30 days, it must be remote. However, it is questionable how effective this really is, although the office, if it does not document them, must remove items within 30 days, in most cases companies will continue to investigate the claims, and when they finally find the proper documentation, the items will be added again.

Whatever you decide regarding a credit repair company, always remember to go over the documents carefully. Also note that credit repair companies cannot legally accept payments until services are completed. They are also required to clearly describe all payments and terms.

The right mindset

Financial problems can be and usually are overwhelming. To make these situations worse, most people do not even know where to begin to solve these financial dilemmas. Basic consumer debt will chain you into slavery, and you could possibly spend your life held down by your own obligations to repay these loans.

The person or institution lending you the money is trusting that you have the ability to hold up your part of the bargain, basically.

Since your ability to repay a loan has been affected, either by the inability to pay or a series of misunderstandings, other lenders will become skeptical when it comes to granting you new credit.

What type of credit should you get? That depends on what you plan to do with the money. The most used types of credit are secured and signature credits. For smaller loans, there's no need for that, as no institution would like to end up with a store of household items, so they lend you money or issue a credit card in your name simply based on the strength of your credit so far.

You can take advantage of budgeting and other techniques, such as debt consolidation, debt settlement, credit counseling, and bankruptcy procedures. You just have to choose the best strategy for you. When choosing from the various options, you have to consider your debt level, your discipline, and plans for the future.

Using Consolidation or Settlement Strategies to Pay Down Debts

Debt consolidation is another strategy that can be used to manage your debts. It involves combining two or more debts at a lower interest rate than you are currently at.

But it is worth doing your research and making some phone calls to see if there is a company that is willing to work with you. If you can lower your monthly bill to a manageable level, at an interest rate that is reasonable, that can make all the difference in handling your debt.

Consolidation and settlement options rose in popularity during the recent financial crisis, appearing in more articles and news pieces than ever before.

Negotiate with Credit Companies

So you are able to take the collection letter they sent you or a past due notice that has been sent to you and discuss it with them. In many cases, they will take a lower amount than what is on the bill just so that they can guarantee they will get some profit.

If you talk to the collection agency and they agree to take a lesser amount, you will have to send that payment in full. Make sure that when you send them the check, you write out the words "paid in full" on the check. Make a copy of the check for your own records as well. Once they cash that check, your account is legally considered to be paid in full and they are no longer able to come after you for more money.

Cut the Credit Cards

Choose a card that will work anywhere, such as a major credit card company.

The best thing to do is make one to two small purchases on your credit card every few months. Try to space out using different cards so that none of them get taken, but do not owe very much money each month.

Talking to Creditors

Tell them the reason why you are having a difficult time paying the debts. Most companies will negotiate a modified payment plan so that monthly payments become more manageable. If you wait for the accounts to go into default, it can and most likely will affect your credit score negatively—which is what we are looking to avoid. Once in default, the collector will start calling.

Credit Counseling

Credit counseling is a service offered by some organizations to borrowers seeking advice on how they can manage their finances. It usually includes budgeting, workshops, and educational resources. A counselor must receive training and certification in budgeting, money and debt management, and consumer credit.

Debt Management Plan

The credit counselor negotiates with the creditors and drafts a payment schedule. Creditors may be amenable to waive some fees or reduce interest rates. Usually, a debt management plan takes about 4 years to be completed, depending on your amount of debt.

Debt Settlement Program

A debt settlement program can be risky, so you have to consider some factors before taking advantage of it. Many of these programs require that you deposit money on an account for at least 3 years before the debt settlement company can settle your debts.

Another aspect to consider is that some creditors will not negotiate for a debt settlement; therefore, the debt settlement company may not be able to pay some of your debts. In addition, some of these debt settlement companies pay off smaller debts first, leaving the large debts to continue growing.

The debt settlement company will suggest that you stop paying your creditors. This decision will result in a significant drop in your credit score. The debts will also incur fees and penalties for nonpayment.

Goodwill Letters

Goodwill letters are not a guaranteed method of removing negative information from your credit report, but are still worth a try in some situations. They are more effective if you have a good history with the company, have had a technical error delayed your payment, or if your autopay did not go through. You can sometimes even convince a credit company to forgive a late payment if you simply forgot to pay.

Try to contact your credit reporting agency by phone to negotiate and explain your situation before sending a goodwill letter. This tactic might be all you need to do in order to remove the record of the late payment. The sooner you contact, the better as well. If you notice that you have a late payment, calling right away could stop it from being reported at all.

To write a goodwill letter you should

Use courteous language that reflects your remorse for the late payment and thank the company for their service.

Include reasons as to why you need to have the record removed, such as qualifying for a home or auto loan or insurance.

- Accept that you were at fault for the late payment.
- Explain what caused the payment to be made late.
- To write a goodwill letter you should not
- Be forceful, rude, or flippant about the situation.

Your financial freedom

Financial freedom is a concept that people love to think about but rarely feel like they can reach. This chapter will help you reach financial freedom by using tips and habits that can be incorporated into your life.

What Does Financial Freedom Mean?

Financial freedom has no set definition. However, it typically means that you are living comfortably and saving for retirement future and your life in general. It can also mean that you have an emergency reserve set up. In general, financial freedom can mean whatever you want it to mean for you. For example, a prior college student may not think that financial freedom includes paying off all their student loans. This is because, at least in this day and age, a college student who needs to pay their own way realizes they will always be paying off their student loans. However, they might feel that student loans are the only debt they should have. Therefore, being able to pay off credit cards or medical bills leads them to financial freedom.

Other people may feel that financial freedom means they are no longer tied down to a job. They are able to live off their savings or a passive income, and they are able to retire and enjoy life through traveling.

Credit Cards and Financial Freedom—Is It Safe?

One of the biggest questions people have when it comes to financial freedom is whether they can have any credit card accounts in their name. While you may not owe anything to your credit cards (in fact, you might only owe one that you pay off in full every month), is this still financial freedom? In general, this is completely determined by your definition of financial freedom. However, if you ever find yourself not being able to pay off your credit card every month, this is not financial freedom. In most cases, financial freedom does mean you no longer have any debt, or at least that you are free from unnecessary debts, such as credit cards.

Most people are quick to state that financial freedom and credit cards do not go together simply because they are not safe with each other. This is due to the fact that it is often easy to fall back into thinking you can pay a certain amount each month and then you become unable to do so. In general, people who reach financial freedom feel that credit cards allow for more of a trap and keep them from ever reaching financial freedom.

The Best Habits to Help You Reach and Protect Your Financial Freedom

When it comes to financial freedom, there are dozens of habits and tips that people provide in order to help you reach your financial freedom. It is important to note that because financial freedom can vary depending on the person's definition, some of the tips and habits might work for you while others may not. You need to find the ones that work best for you, not the ones that other people say are the best.

Make a Budget

Making and keeping a budget is one of the first steps everyone should take while heading towards financial freedom. Even though you might find yourself changing your budget now and then, as you will add or delete bills or receive a different income, you always want to follow it. Not only will this help you in reaching your financial freedom, but continuing to follow your budget will also protect your financial freedom.

Furthermore, creating a monthly budget can help in making sure that all your bills are being paid and you know exactly where your money is going. This will help you know where you can decrease your spending, which will allow you to save more. There are a lot of great benefits when it comes to creating and sticking with a household budget.

Set Up an Automatic Savings Account

If you work for an organization that will automatically place a certain percentage of your check into a savings account, take advantage of this. It gives you the idea that you never had the money to begin with, which means you don't plan for it and you won't find yourself taking the money out of savings unless you need it for an emergency. Furthermore, you can set up a separate savings account where this money will go. You can do it in such a way that you rarely use that account; however, you want to make sure that your money is deposited and everything looks right on your account. But, the whole point of a savings account is not touching it even if you have an emergency, since you will set up an account for emergencies too.

The other idea of this is you pay yourself first. This is often something that people don't think about because they are more worried about paying off their debts.

Keep Your Credit in Mind without Obsessing over It

Your credit score is important, but it is not the most important thing in the world. People often fall into the trap of becoming obsessed over their credit score, especially when they are trying to improve it. One factor to remember is that your credit score is typically only updated every so often. Therefore, you can decide to set time aside every four months to check on your credit report. When you do this, you not only want to check your score, but you also want to check what the CRAs are reporting. Just like you want to make sure everything is correct on your bank account, you want to do the same thing for your credit report.

It Is Fine to Live Below Your Means

One of the biggest factors of financial freedom and being able to maintain it is that you can pay your bills and comfortably live throughout the month. In order to do this, you need to make sure that the money coming into your home is more than the money going out. In other words, you want to live below your means.

This is often difficult for a lot of people because they want to have what other people have. They want to have the newer vehicles, the bigger boat, the newest grill, or anything else. People like to have what their friends and neighbors have. However, one factor people don't think about is that their friends and neighbors probably don't have financial freedom. Therefore, you want to take a moment to think about what is more important to you. Would you rather be in debt like your friends or have financial freedom?

Speak with a Financial Advisor

Sometimes the best step we can take when we are working towards financial freedom is to talk with a financial advisor. They can often give information and help us with a budget, ways to make sure that we get the most out of our income, and also tell us where we might be spending more money than we should. Furthermore, they can help you figure out what the best investments are, which is always helpful when you are looking at financial freedom. At the same time, they can help you plan for your retirement, which is one of the biggest ways in which you can become and remain able to remain financially free.

Completely Pay off Your Credit Cards

If you have high-interest credit cards, which is often the case, you want to make sure that you pay these off every month. Therefore, your credit card spending should become part of your budget. What this means is that you don't want to use your credit card for whatever you feel like. Instead, you want to create a list of where and when you can use your credit card and what you can use it for. For example, you might agree that it is fine in emergency situations or during Christmas shopping. You might also feel that you can use it during trips because it has trip insurance attached to it. Whatever you decide, you want to make sure you follow it.

Track Your Spending

Along with making sure you follow your budget, you also want to track your spending. There are several reasons for this. First, it will help you make sure that your budget is on track. We often forget about automatic bills that are paid monthly or don't realize how much we really spend every month. These factors can affect your budget, which can cause an obstacle when you are working on reaching and keeping your financial freedom.

Fortunately, there are a lot of apps that you can download, many of them are free, which will allow you to easily track your spending. Some of these apps include "Mint" or "Personal Capital." These apps typically give you all the information you need and will automatically tell you how much you are spending and how much income you still hold at the end of the month. Most of these apps will also give you charts to help you see your spending habits in a different way.

Continue Your Education

Another way to stay on top of your financial freedom is to become educated when it comes to your budget, spending, taxes, and anything else to do with your finances. This doesn't mean that you have to go back to school and earn a degree. You can simply do your own research or take online classes—some are low-cost to free. You can also look into webinars that people hold.

You can also help yourself when it comes to investing in the stock market or anything else. There are always several classes you can take online that only have a few sessions or ways you can learn when you have the time. In fact, if you want to invest but don't know what to do or where to begin, one of your best options is to take a class.

Make sure you keep a good mindset while you live financially free. With this mindset, you will not only feel grateful for where you are in life, but you will also remember where you once were. This will help you work towards protecting your financial freedom instead of falling back into credit card debts.

Of course, you can adjust your mindset the way you want to once you reach financial freedom. However, you will want to make sure that you keep your mindset positive. After all, a positive mindset makes you believe that you can accomplish anything.

Make Sure You Write down What Financial Freedom Means to You

Financial freedom can mean something different to you than it means to someone else. Because of this, you have to think about what it truly means to you. Whatever you feel it means, it is important to write this down. This will allow you to turn back to what financial freedom means to you when you find yourself struggling and feeling like you can't gain your financial freedom.

At the same time, it is also helpful to take time to write down your goals. Think of what you want to accomplish on your path to financial freedom. You can also think about what you want to do after you have reached financial freedom. Give yourself goals to work towards, as this will help you stay on track better.

The Best Habits to Help You Reach and Protect Your Financial Freedom

When it comes to financial freedom, there are dozens of habits and tips that people provide in order to help you reach your financial freedom. It is important to note that because financial freedom can vary depending on the person's definition, some of the tips and habits might work for you while others may not. You need to find the ones that work best for you, not the ones that other people say are the best. Therefore, I am going to give you a fairly large list as I want you to make sure that you can find some of the best habits and tips so you can not only reach financial freedom but also protect it.

Make a Budget

Making and keeping a budget is one of the first steps everyone should take while heading towards your financial freedom. Even though you might find yourself changing your budget now and then, as you will add or delete bills or receive a different income, you always want to follow it. Not only will this help you in reaching your financial freedom but continuing to follow your budget will also protect your financial freedom.

Furthermore, creating a monthly budget can make sure that all your bills are being paid and you know exactly where your money is going. For example, you will be able to see how much money you spend on groceries, gas, and eating out at restaurants. This will help you know where you can decrease your spending, which will allow you to save more. There are a lot of great benefits when it comes to creating and sticking with a household budget.

Set Up Automatic Savings Account

If you work for an organization that will automatically place a certain percentage of your check into a savings account, take advantage of this. It gives you the idea that you never had the money to begin with, which means you don't plan for it and you won't find yourself taking the money out of savings unless you need it for an emergency. Furthermore, you can set up a separate savings account where this money will go. You can make it, so you rarely see this account, however, you want to make sure that your money is deposited, and everything looks right on your account. But, the point of this account if you do not touch it, even if you have an emergency. Instead, you will set up a different account for emergency basis.

The other idea to this is you pay yourself first. This is often something that people don't think about because they are more worried about paying off their debt. However, many financial advisors say that you are always number one when it comes to your finances. While you want to pay your bills, you also need to make sure that you and your family are taken care of.

Keep Your Credit in Mind Without Obsessing Over It

Your credit score is important, but it is not the most important thing in the world. People often fall into the trap of becoming obsessed over their credit score, especially when they are trying to improve it. One factor to remember is that your credit score is typically only updated every so often. Therefore, you can decide to set time aside every quarter to check on your credit report. When you do this, you not only want to check your score, but you also want to check what the credit bureaus are reporting. Just like you want to make sure everything is correct on your bank account; you want to do the same thing for your credit report.

It Is Fine to Live Below Your Means

One of the biggest factors of financial freedom and being able to maintain it is you can make your bills and comfortably live throughout the month. In order to do this, you need to make sure that the money coming into your home is more than the money going out. In other words, you want to live below your means.

This is often difficult for a lot of people because they want to have what other people have. They want to have the newer vehicles, the bigger boat, the newest grill, or anything else. People like to have what their friends and neighbors have. However, one-factor people don't think about is that their friends and neighbors probably don't have financial freedom. Therefore, you want to take a moment to think about what is more important for you. Would you rather be in debt like your friends or you would rather have financial freedom?

Speak with a Financial Advisor

Sometimes the best steps we can take when we are working towards financial freedom is to talk with a financial advisor. They can often give up information and help us with a budget, ways to make sure that we get the most out of our income, and also tell us where we might be spending more money than we should. Furthermore, they can help you figure out what the best investments are, which are always helpful when you are looking at financial freedom. At the same time, they can help you plan for your retirement, which is one of the biggest ways you will be able to remain financially free.

Completely Pay Off Your Credit Cards

If you are high-interest credit cards, which is often the case, you want to make sure that you pay these off every month. Therefore, your credit card spending should become part of your budget. What this means is you don't want to use your credit card for whatever you feel like. Instead, you want to create a list on when you can and when you can't use your credit card. For example, you might agree that it is fine in emergency situations or during Christmas shopping. You might also feel that you can use it during tips because it has trip insurance attached to it. Whatever you decide, you want to make sure you follow.

You also want to make sure that you pay off any high-interest loans. When it comes to loans that are lower in interest, they won't affect you too much.

Track Your Spending

Along with making sure you follow your budget; you also want to track your spending. There are several reasons for this. First, it will help you make sure that your budget is on track. We often forget about automatic bills that are paid monthly or don't realize how much we really spend every month. These factors can make our budget off, which can cause an obstacle when you are working to reaching and keeping your financial freedom.

Fortunately, there are a lot of apps that you can download, many of them are free, which will allow you to track your spending easily. Some of these apps include Mint or Personal Capital. These apps typically give you all the information you need and will automatically tell you how much you are spending and how much income you still hold at the end of the month. Most of these apps will also give you charts to help you see your spending habits in a different way.

Make Sure to Keep Your Mindset

This is a mindset that you will want to continue to have while you are living financially free. With this mindset, you will not only feel grateful for where you are in life, but you will also remember where you once were. This will help you work towards protecting your financial freedom instead of falling back into credit card debt.

Of course, you can adjust your mindset the way you want to once you reach financial freedom. However, you will want to make sure that you keep your mindset positive. After all, a positive mindset makes you believe that you can accomplish anything.

The 5 best ways to pay off debts

Your credit use rate or the aggregate sum of accessible debt utilized on your accounts (unsecured and secured) is the second biggest factor toward obtaining a solid credit score. Beside your verified debt, which is paid down according to a calendar and doesn't increase in the amount owed, we should concentrate here on uncollateralized debt, which is the costliest debt and furthermore, the debt that is least demanding to gain out of power. In case you're overpowered with debt or have burrowed a huge gap from which you're uncertain how to begin moving out, my first advice is to unwind. There is absolutely no motivation to experience the ill effects of superfluous uneasiness or stress in light of debt. Losing rest and agonizing night and day over fortuitous debt won't assist you with receiving in return, so accept the way that you are in debt and start considering how and when you can receive in return.

Credit Card Debt is the Costliest Debt

Credit card debt is the most choking out debt of all, and the feeling of always digging and getting no place is a feeling to which I can relate very well. Don't give it a chance to make you crazy. With an activity plan and being persevering not to overextend yourself, you can gradually arrive at a point where your credit card debt is neither bringing you nor your credit score down. While I'm not a specialist in credit card debt guiding.

I realize that in my circumstance, I had the option to toss little lumps of my compensation at this pile of debt — a few months in bigger pieces, others in littler pieces—until I had a little enough balance to clear out. While this segment intends to provide some accommodating tips on the most proficient method to manage your debt, if that you believe you are absolutely up the creek without a paddle, or a significant life event, for example, joblessness, or a medicinal issue or anything is preventing you from having the option to pay down any of your debt, at that point jumping to the following segment might be progressively appropriate for you.

Debt Management Tips

For those of you who are in the limbo period of, "Should I pay-down debt," or "Should I file bankruptcy," comprehend that there are two types of personal bankruptcy: the main, Bankruptcy, takes into consideration most or the entirety of your debts to be discharged or dropped. The second, known as Bankruptcy, plans your debt for repayment over some stretch of time. If that you are thinking about both two choices, at that point it is highly recommended that you search out somebody with mastery, for example, a bankruptcy trustee or lawyer. Sometimes everything necessary is a professional's advice and helping hand to guide you the correct way. If you are going to attempt to dig yourself out of debt without documenting personal bankruptcy or choosing your debts for not exactly the aggregate sum owed with your creditors, you have to have a plan.

What's the Best Approach to Deal with Huge Credit Card Debt?

There is no uncertainty that the interest on credit card debt can be an executioner. Many credit cards have interest rates more than 20%. If you utilize Chris' Debt Repayment Calculator (at welker.ca) you can perceive the amount it will cost to pay off your credit cards with interest more than five years. Perhaps the biggest error that people make when they are attempting to dig themselves out of debt all alone is making payments that simply spread the interest charges yet aren't really lessening the head.

Chris Walker says that if you are battling to deal with your credit card debt and you need to pay back what you can bear, at that point the best alternative may be a consumer proposal for a repayment. By offering a consumer proposal, you can stop interest charges, prevent creditor collection activity, and settle your debt. While documenting a consumer proposal briefly damages your credit rating, it is frequently the best approach for people dealing with huge credit card debt. Don't make the mistake of concentrating on your credit rating. While credit rating is important, improving your financial wellbeing is undeniably progressively important. You can generally modify your credit rating, yet If that you don't have a plan to escape debt you will continue to battle.

If You Need to Manage Your Credit Card APRs

In cases of medical or employment hardships, or some other setbacks in life, creditors will sometimes permit a decrease or freeze on additional fund charges to your existing debt. Everything necessary is calling to discover what they can do subsequent to disclosing to them your circumstance—it might be critical enough to accommodate their explanation codes or extraordinary programs. Creditors frequently save these for people who might be not able make timely payments or the full amount of the average monthly payments due, and the programs may keep going for set time periods of six months to a year or more.

In return for enrolling in these programs, a few creditors may likewise stop your account preventing you from making additional buys and adding to your existing debt. Obviously, you won't realize what options you have until you call, so in case you're reluctant about grabbing the telephone, discover the time to call every one of your creditors and examine these options which could bring some truly necessary help. Inquire as to whether you can make a lesser monthly payment. This would be your most solid option If that you are as yet ready to manage a smidgen of a monthly payment, notwithstanding any plans for a DIY debt settlement. You'll be happy you called — anything to help diminish the amount of interest charged and APRs consistently. The goal here is to get what, assuming any, options you have, at managing or keeping your balances low. Twofold check that by enrolling yourself in any diminished APR or APR-freezing programs, creditors will continue reporting to the CRAs that you are making timely payments. (Creditors can begin reporting harsh payments if a bill is 30days overdue.)

Settling Your Own Debts

While personal debt settlement was to a great extent a totally unbelievable practice as meagre as five years back, a plenty of DIY debt pilgrims have now taken their accounts of the process to online media and web journals. More news and research on the subject, by and large, has additionally now put the process inside go after the individuals who wish to take the creditors head-on. Many have picked this course to be in all out control of their settlement process as opposed to enlisting an outsider debt arbitrator to intercede. You can settle your debts all alone; anyway, you should be prepared and solid willed. You'll need to suffer and confront creditors' and debt collectors' endeavors and strategies at getting you to pay up, which can be out and out forceful and smooth. Furthermore, you will must be sorted out at managing and monitoring the results of each arranged account. People are procured by organizations to make debt collection their full-time exertion and are compensated accordingly, so don't overlook they are professionals at endeavoring to get anything they can out of any debtor.

Debt settlement is positively an option for any individual who basically can't make payments or who has fallen so behind that the subsequent stage would resort bankruptcy. An outline of personal debt settlement includes:

Halting any payments on every uncollateralized debt that you can't pay. Right away.

Pausing and avoiding creditors as they attempt to chase you down to collect their outstanding payments. If that they have your telephone number, it is alright getting another PDA saved for loved ones. The goal is released the account until it gets so far financially past due that they will be desperate to settle with you before charging off the account.

Proposing a debt settlement for as meager as 20 percent on the amount you owe. This may require some intense arrangement and standing your ground.

Affirming everything in writing from the creditor regarding any debt settlement and payback terms. It is prudent to not fall for a reset of the process by sending in any cash until you have, in your grasp, the creditor's letter plotting the terms which are agreeable to you.

Once more, personal debt settlement isn't for everybody. Debt settlement will assuredly damage your credit when creditors and collection agencies continue reporting reprobate payments on your accounts.

You'll get a good deal on any charges you'd pay debt directing or combination organizations to consult for your sake. Likewise, you may have an easier time with creditors, since your creditors and collectors will realize they're dealing straightforwardly with you rather than an agent, who might be harder to work with. Creditors may go easier on you.

Credit score myths to unlearn

For a large portion of credit scoring's history, by far, most of the people engaged with loaning decisions pretty much needed to think about what hurt or helped a score. Makers of scoring formulas would not like to uncover much about how the models functioned, for dread that contenders would take their thoughts or that consumers would make sense of how to beat the framework. Luckily, today we discover much increasingly about credit scoring—however, not every person has stayed aware of the latest knowledge. Mortgage intermediaries, loan officials, credit agency agents, credit guides, and the media, among others, continue to spread outdated and out and out bogus information.

Loans have become a great tool that helps people solve their financial issues in no time. Although, beyond the several advantages and responsibilities, there are certain myths that we must be aware of and break. If you have plans to acquire a loan but are not sure if it's your best option.

While some of us like credit score as it has favored us in our ability to handle it well, others see it as one that does more harm than good, which is not the case. The issue with people who do not enjoy the credit score is because they were misinformed on some things and it leads them to fall into traps they could have avoided if they had the right information all along.

Following up on their terrible guidance can put your score and your accounts at critical risk.

Closing Credit Accounts Will Help Your Score

This one sounds sensible, particularly when a mortgage merchant discloses to you that lenders are suspicious of people who have heaps of unused credit accessible to them. All What's you, all things considered, from hurrying out and charging up a tempest? Obviously, looking at the situation objectively, what's shielded you from piling on huge balances before now? If you've been responsible with credit before, you're probably going to continue to be responsible later. That is the essential standard behind credit scoring: Its rewards practices that show moderate, responsible utilization of credit after some time, because those propensities are probably going to continue.

The score likewise rebuffs conduct that is not all that responsible, for example, applying for a lot of credit you don't require. Numerous people with high credit scores locates that one of only a handful hardly any detriments for them is the number of credit accounts recorded on their reports. At the point when they go to get their credit scores, they're informed that one reason their score isn't considerably higher is that they have "too many open accounts." Many mistakenly expect they can "fix" this issue by closing accounts. In any case, after you've opened the accounts, you've done the damage. You can't fix it by closing the account. You can, however, make matters more awful.

You Can Increase Your Score by Asking Your Credit Card Company to Lower Your Limits

This one is a minor departure from the possibility that decreasing your accessible credit by one way or another enables your score by making you to appear to be less risky to lenders. By and by, it's missing the goal. Narrowing the difference between the credit you use and the credit you have accessible to you can negatively affect your score. It doesn't make a difference that you requested the decrease; the FICO formula doesn't recognize lower limits that you mentioned and lower limits forced by a creditor. All it sees is less difference between your balances and your limits, and that is not good. If that, you need to enable your score, to handle the issue from the opposite end: by paying down your debt. Expanding the gap between your balance and your credit limit positively affects your score.

You Need to Pay Interest to Obtain a Good Credit Score

This is the precise inverse of the past myth, and it's similarly as misinformed. It is not necessary for you to carry a balance on your credit cards and pay interest to have a good score. As you've perused a few times as of now, your credit reports—and subsequently the FICO formula—make no differentiation between balances you carry month to month and balances that you pay off. Savvy consumers don't carry credit card balances under any circumstances, and not to improve their scores. Presently, the facts confirm that to get the highest FICO scores, you must have both revolving accounts, for example, credit cards, and instalment loans, for example, a mortgage or car loan. What's more, except for those 0 per cent rates used to drive auto deals after Sept. 11, most instalment loans require paying interest.

Yet, here's a news streak: You don't have to have the highest score to get good credit. Any score more than 720 or so will get you the best rates and terms with numerous lenders. A few, particularly auto and home value lenders, save their best bargains for those with scores more than 760. You don't must have an 850, or even 800 score, to get incredible arrangements. In case you're attempting to improve a fair score, a little, reasonable instalment loan can help—if you can get affirmed for it and pay it off on time. However, some way or another, there's no motivation to stray into the red and pay interest.

Your Closed Accounts Should Indicate "Closed by Consumer," Or They Will Hurt Your Score

The hypothesis behind this myth is that lenders will see a closed account on your credit report and, if not educated generally, will accept that a nauseated creditor cut you off because you botched in some way or another. Obviously, as you most likely are aware at this point, numerous lenders never observe your real report. They're simply taking a gander at your credit score, which couldn't care less who closed a credit card. Fair Isaac figures that if a lender closes your account, it's either for dormancy or because you defaulted. If that you defaulted, that will be sufficiently archived in the account's history. If it makes you feel better to contact the bureaus and guarantee that accounts you closed are recorded as "closed by consumer," by all methods do as such. However, it won't make any distinction to your credit score.

Credit Counseling Is Way Worse Than Bankruptcy

Sometimes this is expressed as "credit advising is as awful as bankruptcy" or "credit directing is as terrible as bankruptcy." None of these statements is valid. A bankruptcy recording is the single most noticeably terrible thing you can do to your credit score. On the other hand, the current FICO formula totally ignores any reference to credit guiding that may be on your credit report. Credit guiding is treated as an impartial factor, neither aiding nor hurting your score. Credit guides, if you're inexperienced with the term, have practical experience in arranging lower interest rates and also working out payment plans for debtors that may some way or another file for bankruptcy. Although credit advisors may consolidate the consumer's bills into one monthly payment, they don't give loans—as debt consolidators do—or guarantee to wipe out or settle debts for not exactly the chief amount you owe.

The fact that credit guiding itself won't affect your score doesn't mean, notwithstanding, that enrolling in a credit advisor's debt management plan will leave your credit sound. A few lenders will report you as late only for enrolling in a debt management plan. Their thinking is that you're not paying them what you initially owed, so you ought to need to endure some agony. That is not, by any means, the only way you could be reported late. Not all credit instructors are made equivalent, and some have been blamed for retaining consumer payments that were proposed for creditors.

When You Close Your Many Credit Accounts, Your Credit Score Will Improve

This may seem logically sound but is completely false. The way credit scores are calculated is in parts known as credit/ debt ratio. The agencies who calculate your score evaluate the amount of debt that you have and the amount of credit that is available for you to draw.

So let's assume you have 10 credit cards and the credit availability all sums up to $100,000 and you have used only $15,000 of that available credit, your credit utilization rate becomes 15%. This is known as positive since you have 85% of your unused credit.

Let's take a case of you closing seven accounts because you're not using them. You will still have $15,000 in debt but in this case, your sum total credit now available drops to $30,000. This means that your credit utilization rate has skyrocketed by 50%, hence your credit score dropping.

Do not close credit cards like this. It is better to put the cards away safely. And if there's a chance you can increase your credit limit, go for it. As long as you are not maximizing it, it will help your credit score.

One Thing That Affects Your Score Is The Amount Of Money You Make.

This is so not true. Your credit score does not list the employers' income but rather the credit accounts. So regardless of what you earn a year; whether you're a CEO who earns 3 million a year or an entry-level worker who earns $30,000 a year, your income does not determine your credit score. Interestingly, a wealthy CEO, even with so much money, might have a bad credit score because of bankruptcy or successions of late payments in the earlier years.

The only way that your income can affect your credit score is if you live a Champagne lifestyle and having only a beer budget. That can be financially unhealthy for you. If it happens that you run out of your cards, by making minimum payments and losing them completely, your score gradually becomes a great success and peaks the top, as it should.

Credit Scores Tend To Change Only A Few Times A Year

Credit scores are usually in constant change. The information with which you calculate your score is derived from the financial institutions you maintain business relationships with. If you miss making a payment, it will reflect almost immediately. If you go ahead to close multiple accounts, the information will have an impact on your score much earlier than 3 or 6 months.

Looking at your credit score now, you can be able to see the latest updates that have been made. The time actually varies as sometimes it can be a matter of hours, than days or even weeks. Knowing this, you should ensure to check your credit score on a regular basis. So in case something bad happens, you can address it early enough.

Once You Have A Bad Credit Score, It Is Impossible To Get Loans Or Credits

This myth has been derived from advertisements that require a good credit score to get funding. Interestingly, almost everyone can get funding no matter what their credit score may be; whether it is increased in the 800s or lower in the 400s.

What a credit score represents to financial institutions is a level of risk as this determines to a large extent the terms of any loan or credit received. Let's say for example someone who has a credit score of 800, the individual will be considered low risk for the financial institution. They already know that this person pays in good time, has available credit in high quantity and has longevity with his accounts. This will hence result in a low-interest rate and more credit available.

However, someone with a credit score of 450 will be considered a high-risk. The reason is that the loans and credits will be available but will have oppressive interest rates for very few credits.

You Can Have An Excellent Credit Report If You Have No Credit

The lack of credit is a good thing in some countries but not in the US. If you have never had a credit card or a car loan, you must be financially responsible. But as for the United States, your credit history determines your credit score. Good credit history equals a good credit score and vice versa.

All in all, credit scores are built. Financial institutions who lend loans and credits want to know that you will borrow money and payback on time coupled with an interest. Once they see that, then you are safe from any risk.

Bringing A Balance To Your Credit Card Also Helps Your Score

No, not at all. To be quite frank, it doesn't hurt that either. But you would be wrong to think that keeping money on your card helps your score because it really doesn't. Ideally, I advise you to pay the balances on your cards fully every month in order to avoid paying interest on purchases. If you're just paying the minimum, then you're not doing yourself any good and wasting your money. Most of this minimum payment can be paid to the credit card company as only a small fraction pays the balance.

Do not bring a balance, whenever possible. And if your balance exceeds 30% of your card, you should consider transferring from half to another card. When one-third of the credit is used on a card, then that can actually damage the credit score. In an ideal case, the balance ought to be less than 30% of the credit available; the lower it is, the better for you. This will be a good place to request for a credit line increase so as your line is increased by a few thousand dollars, your balance is affected and falls below 30%, hence increasing your credit score.

You Can't Recover From A Bad Credit Score. It Stays With You For Life.

If you are one currently has a poor score, it is not the end of the world. If you are paying exorbitant interest rates now, you won't be doing so forever. Although, repairing and rebuilding take time and patience.

Stick with the basics and be consistent with it. Open new credit lines and pay your credit card bills in time. Try never to miss a payment. Make your balances low at all times. Keep a very steady but low credit usage ratio. Do not apply to many cards or accounts in a year.

Once you can do these, even amidst all financial difficulties, your credit score will change for better.

Breakdown of the credit stages and phases

The road to re-establishing your credit can be a bumpy one, especially if you have to start over from scratch. The main thing you want to remember is that you need to have a solid foundation to rebuild your reputation. Several basic guidelines can help you to stay on course.

Whatever your goals are, once your credit report has got the boost that it needs, the efforts to reestablish your credit should begin with you. While you may have big dreams, you need to recover slowly. You don't want to make a misstep and end up falling back down the rabbit hole again.

Often, after having a rough bout with credit, the tendency is to swear off credit for good. The vow to go strictly cash can be strong after surviving a difficult time with creditors and bill collectors. However, that is not always a wise decision. In fact, it could make it even more difficult for you later on. You've learned your lesson about bad credit, but you are smarter now, and you know that credit itself is not the bad guy, it's how you use it.

You now have a credit goal, and you know what to do with it. You know how much credit you can charge and still keep your score high, and you know the importance of making timely payments. You have all the tools you need in your arsenal to start your rebuilding campaign.

Know How Much Credit You Need

This will give you a general idea of just how much credit you should have.

For this, you need to determine your debt to income ratio. When you are ready to apply for new credit, lenders will look at this percentage to make a final decision on giving you credit.

The formula for this is simple. Take the total from your list of financial obligations and divide it by your gross monthly income. It will give you the percentage of credit you should have in your arsenal. For example, if your monthly income is $1500.00 and your total monthly expenses are $800, the formula should look something like this:

$800/1500 = 53\%$

The higher this percentage is, the less likely a creditor will be willing to grant you new credit, even with a good score.

Start Small

You may have big dreams but keep them within realistic boundaries. Remember, you're trying to recover from credit illness. If you had been physically ill to the point where you needed hospitalization, you wouldn't come home from the hospital and automatically resume your same routine. You will build up your strength a little at a time until you were back to the same physical condition you were before.

You should view rebuilding your credit in the same way. Don't look to establish an unsecured bank credit card fresh out of the gate—these are probably the most difficult to get.

When filling out your application, here are a few things to keep in mind to make the process go smoother so that the results will lean more in your favor.

Do not put in more than three applications for credit in a single month. More than that and your score will drop.

Don't add anything to your application that won't benefit you in some way. Some businesses will allow you to make purchases without established credit, but will only report to the CRA once you've paid it off. Only put these on your application if you've made regular payments and you know it will boost your score.

As the months go by and you are making regular payments, you can begin to increase your purchase amounts little by little. Your creditor will notice that you are spending wisely and will probably drop the need for security behind the card you have, and perhaps even increase your limit. Remember, they make their money by charging interest so the more money you borrow, the more they can earn. Still, you don't have credit to support them, so maintain self-control and stay within your limits and your score will naturally increase.

Protect What You Have

No matter how much or how little credit you have, never take it for granted. Make sure that you follow the rules and your credit should stay in good condition.

With revolving credit (credit cards), avoid using them too often. Only spend as much as you can reasonably pay off within a given month. No doubt, you will continue to hit rough patches here and there, even people with good credit need to be prepared. With the credit card that you use infrequently, make it a habit of making a small purchase from time to time so that the account does not become inactive. Then pay off the total balance immediately when you do.

Establish a rapport with your creditors. That way, if you end up paying late one month, you have a friend you can call to help you to recover quickly. Missing a payment or paying late can be the death knell for a newly recovered credit score. The more friends you have in your corner, the more likely you will come out on top when that happens.

Use automation whenever you can. We all lead busy lives, and it can be easy for a date to pass by without you noticing it. One way to do this is to use modern technology to your advantage by taking advantage of automated payment systems. This will ensure that every payment will be made on time without you having to worry about it.

There Are Several Ways to Do This

It is pretty easy to make up automatic payment arrangements through any of these plans, but arranging it directly with your creditor is probably the fastest and simplest way to do it.

A word of caution: If you decide to make this arrangement through your bank, you will always have to make sure that your account has enough balance to make the payment. This can start an ugly domino effect that could threaten to undermine all the efforts you've made to get your credit back on top.

This decision works best for those who have a regular monthly income that they can be sure will be in their bank at the right time. At the end of the day, the main goal is to never be late or miss a payment so you can avoid falling behind and running into a lot more problems than you bargained for.

You're in It for the Long Haul

When you're under a lot of pressure from collection agencies and creditors, it is easy to think that repairing credit and getting back on track is an emergency, but your credit will be with you for the long term. There will be some things you won't be able to address immediately, and you will have to wait it out.

Don't rush the process; take your time and be methodical in your approach, and the chances of your clearing up your good name are quite good.

Focus on the future, not the immediate present, and you will be driven to make sure that every step you take will be sustainable and you will be able to establish and maintain your new credit score for the years to come.

Conclusion

After reading this plan you have to come up with a financial plan which will help you start to pay off your credit cards strategically. You then have to make sure that, no matter what, you follow this plan. Even if you find yourself in an emergency after a few months when your car breaks down, you should find another way to come up with your emergency funding. It is important that you continue to make more than the minimum payment on time with all your credit cards. The fewer fees you need to add into your balance, the quicker you will be able to pay off your credit card debt.

Another way to bring down credit card debt quickly, especially if you are overdrawn and missed a few payments, is to contact the credit card company. While many people don't realize this, most credit card companies want to work with you. The number one reason for this is they want to keep you as a customer, basically, so they can continue receiving your money. One strategy to use is to call and say that you would like to close your account. They will then try to focus on keeping your account open, which usually results in them dropping a few missed payment or over the limit fees. Another strategy to use is simply to explain to them what happened, why you were late, and tell them that you want to put your account in good standing. They are usually willing to drop some fees or so much money if you are willing to pay a certain amount off that day.

Don't hesitate, put all the notions of the book into practice immediately and improve your credit score!

CPSIA information can be obtained
at www.ICGtesting.com
Printed in the USA
BVHW031010280421
606021BV00001B/9